VOLUME 91 • NUMBER 2 • SUMMER 2002

# NATIO CIVIC REVIEW

## MAKING CITIZEN DEMOCRACY WORK

IN THIS ISSUE

# Issues in Democratic Politics: Public Deliberation, Electoral Reform, and Civic Participation

Christopher T. Gates
*President, National Civic League*

Robert Loper
*Editor*

A Publication of the National Civic League and Jossey-Bass

NATIONAL CIVIC REVIEW (ISSN 0027-9013) is published quarterly by Wiley Subscription Services, Inc., A Wiley Company, at Jossey-Bass, 989 Market Street, San Francisco, CA 94103-1741, and the National Civic League, 1445 Market Street, Suite 300, Denver, CO 80202-1717. NCL, founded in 1894 as the National Municipal League, advocates a new civic agenda to create communities that work for everyone. NCL is a 501(c)(3) nonprofit, non-partisan educational association of individuals and organizations. NCL members have access to the information and services necessary to improve community life. For complete information, contact Derek Okubo, (303) 571-4343.

INDEXED in Public Affairs Information Service, ABC POL SCI, and Book Review Index.

SUBSCRIPTIONS are $55.00 per year for individuals and $105.00 per year for institutions. To order subscriptions, single issues, or reprints, please refer to the Ordering Information page at the back of this issue.

PERIODICALS postage paid at San Francisco, California, and at additional mailing offices. POSTMASTER: send address changes to *National Civic Review*, Jossey-Bass Inc., 989 Market Street, San Francisco, CA 94103-1741.

NCL MEMBERS send change of address to Debbie Gettings, National Civic League, 1445 Market Street, Suite 300, Denver, CO 80202-1717.

EDITORIAL CORRESPONDENCE should be sent to Robert Loper, National Civic League, 1319 F Street NW, Suite 204, Washington, DC 20004.

www.josseybass.com

ISBN: 978-0-7879-6362-0

LETTERS TO THE EDITOR. *National Civic Review* welcomes letters to the editor. Write to *National Civic Review*, 1319 F Street, Suite 204, Washington, DC 20004, or send e-mail to robert@ncldc.org. Please include your name, address, and telephone number.

# CONTENTS

NOTE FROM THE PRESIDENT                                                    115
*Christopher T. Gates*

ARTICLES

Deliberative Dialogue to Expand Civic Engagement:
What Kind of Talk Does Democracy Need?                                     117
*Martha L. McCoy, Patrick L. Scully*

> Public deliberation is widely recognized as essential to a well-
> functioning democracy. Officials from the Study Circles Resource
> Center identify essential principles of deliberative dialogue linked to
> political engagement.

Enlisting Citizens: Building Political Legitimacy                          137
*Matt Leighninger*

> Statewide deliberative projects in Oklahoma, Minnesota, and New
> York offer valuable lessons for involving citizens in public decision
> making.

Public Participation in Environmental Decision Making:
Is It Working?                                                             149
*Matthew McKinney, Will Harmon*

> Officials from the Montana Consensus Council report on an assess-
> ment of public participation in environmental policymaking in Mon-
> tana and provide recommendations for improving the quality of such
> involvement.

Trends in Philanthropy: Democracy as Homeland Security                     171
*David Mathews*

> The president of the Kettering Foundation describes a civil investment
> initiative among foundations to rethink grantmaking procedures and
> target ways of supporting civic learning.

Changing Channels: How the Nonprofit Sector Can Help
Improve Local Television News                                              185
*Sean P. Treglia*

> With the coming move from analog to digital broadcasting, commer-
> cial broadcasters may no longer be under any obligation to provide
> news that serves the public interest. However, the nonprofit sector
> may be able to guide commercial electronic media toward improve-
> ments in the quality of television news that are also commercially
> viable.

Fixing Elections: The Failure of America's Winner-Take-All Politics        193
*Steven Hill*

> Majoritarian elections are having many deleterious effects on voter
> participation and representation.

Big Wins for Democracy: San Francisco and Vermont
Vote for Instant Runoff Voting                                    201
*Eric C. Olson, Steven Hill*

> Instant runoff voting continues to attract interest and victories
> at the polls.

States and Campaign Finance Reform                                205
*David Schultz*

> A review of the growing impact of money on state-level campaigns
> and elections concludes that disclosure laws should be complemented
> by public financing mechanisms.

# NOTE FROM THE PRESIDENT

Much of the National Civic League's work in communities was developed over the same period in which policymaking authority and responsibility were being devolved from the federal government to state and local governments. As communities adapted to the challenge of meeting new obligations, the need to change how they did business became apparent. With its stress on governance and the development of new roles for citizens, businesses, governments, and nonprofits, NCL's approach to community building and citizen democracy found a receptive audience.

Of course, NCL was far from alone in stepping up to help communities understand and improve how local political decisions are made. The past several decades have seen impressive growth in the number and sophistication of community-oriented movements and local intermediary organizations, some of which were described in volume 90, number 4 of NCR, published in 2001. Collaborative processes and consensus-building techniques are now in widespread use in communities across the country.

While this reinvigoration of civic engagement is encouraging, it is clear that much remains to be done. The resources and political will required to ensure homeland security, improve educational outcomes, and provide access to affordable health care must be drawn from all sectors of society. ·

Political reform is like repairing a leaky boat while on the water—you can't replace everything all at once. Our belief at NCL is that sustainable political reform begins at the state and local levels. But this focus is not meant to preclude engagement with national politics. As we in the reform community seek to reengage citizens and renew political institutions, we must develop ways of more effectively connecting political activity at the local level with ongoing national debates. This issue of NCR takes up this goal and contains articles on a number of important reform ideas and issues.

One of the most promising ways to improve how public decisions are made is to engage more citizens in the dialogue surrounding community decision-making processes. Forums for public deliberation are one of the best means of convening local dialogues on political issues that affect communities across the country. In a pair of companion articles in this issue, practitioners from the Study Circles Resource Center detail the conceptual underpinnings of deliberative dialogue and describe the outcomes of several statewide deliberative projects. An article by officials of the Montana Consensus Council complements this perspective and presents an analysis of public participation in environmental decision making in Montana.

Foundations also have an essential role to play in broadening the reach and deepening the impact of democratic discourse in the United States. The president of the Kettering Foundation, David Mathews, offers his ideas on how philanthropy can support deliberation to further democracy's mission of self-rule expressed through collective action. Accurate and reliable information is a prerequisite for deliberation, and the importance of keeping citizens informed is given an interesting twist in an article by Sean P. Treglia of the Pew Charitable Trust. Treglia calls for cooperation between the nonprofit sector and commercial media to make the case that high-quality news broadcasts can be economically successful. Finally, passage in San Francisco this spring of a proposition endorsing the use of instant run-off voting underscores the importance of voting reforms for widening participation.

The great Austrian economist Joseph Schumpeter memorably linked the productive capacities of capitalism to a process of creative destruction. Paraphrasing this notion, we can identify creative adaptation as the wellspring for the productive forces of democracy. Democratic renewal is a work in progress. Over the years complacency and narrow self-concern have attenuated the bonds of community in our country. Our present circumstances in the continuing disquiet of this new and never-to-be-innocent century make unfamiliar demands on us. While the rich associational life that characterized our past can provide some inspiration, it does not present a model that is adequate to the new challenges we face. We must develop new, more inclusive forms of community that will support the responsibilities of self-governance to which we are obligated. We think that the ideas expressed in the articles composing this issue have a valuable role in this collective endeavor.

CHRISTOPHER T. GATES
PRESIDENT, NATIONAL CIVIC LEAGUE

# Deliberative Dialogue to Expand Civic Engagement: What Kind of Talk Does Democracy Need?

*Martha L. McCoy, Patrick L. Scully*

The need to expand and deepen civic engagement is a central theme of a loosely defined and growing civic movement. A strong civic life and a flourishing democracy presume the active involvement of many people across society. Civic engagement is thus both a barometer of our public life and a focal point for action when we want to improve it. While regular citizen-to-citizen communication has always been a central part of democracy, public deliberation is just starting to be defined as a field of thought and practice. In this article we focus on face-to-face democratic deliberation as a means of enhancing civic engagement.

We bring ideas and insights from our work in communities to answer the question, "What kind of public talk is most likely to expand civic engagement and make it meaningful to all sorts of people?" This emerging field has a rich and growing set of perspectives and practices; unfortunately, we don't have the space to catalogue and detail all the promising approaches and what they have taught us. But we can describe what we have been learning in communities where community-wide deliberation for action and change is being used as a process for widespread, meaningful civic engagement. In doing this we make a case for two powerful but unusual marriages that are frequently missing when public talk is used to strengthen civic engagement.

The first union is between two strains of public talk—dialogue and deliberation. The process of *dialogue,* as it is usually understood, can bring many benefits to civic life—an orientation toward constructive communication, the dispelling of stereotypes, honesty in relaying ideas, and the intention to listen to and understand the other.[1] A related process, *deliberation,* brings a different benefit—the use of critical thinking and reasoned argument as a way for citizens to make decisions on public policy. We will describe what we have learned about how the combination of deliberation and dialogue can be used

*Note:* The authors would like to thank Molly Holme Barrett for her superb editorial advice.

to create mutual understanding and connect personal with public concerns. People use this type of public conversation, what we term deliberative dialogue,[2] to build relationships, solve public problems, and address policy issues.

The second critical marriage is between community organizing and deliberative dialogue. Frequently, those who use some form of public talk focus only on the characteristics of the talk itself. When they speak about effectiveness, they describe the quality of the dialogue or the deliberation "inside the circle." While that is important, it isn't enough. Whenever public talk is being used for civic engagement—that is, to involve people in addressing public problems—it is critical to create a wider context for the conversation. In addition to focusing on how people will be brought into the conversation, it is essential to address how the community context of the conversation will be structured so that the conversation can have an impact on public life. In this article we also describe what we have learned about the kind of community-wide organizing that makes deliberative dialogue effective for community building and public problem solving.[3]

We hope that our description of this kind of public talk and its connection to community organizing will be useful not only to anyone using deliberation and dialogue for civic engagement but also to those using other kinds of civic engagement processes. Our goal is to make transparent our assumptions and working principles for effective civic engagement. By describing what we are learning, we hope to spark a larger and more comprehensive conversation among theorists and practitioners about the connection of deliberative dialogue to some of the key goals and questions of the civic movement.

## Making and Strengthening Civic Connections: The Search for Effective Processes

Most people do not enter community life or politics through doors marked "civic life" or "engagement." Instead, they find themselves inside after they start working on an issue about which they care deeply. Once they try to make progress on the issue, they realize that they need to engage other people in finding and implementing solutions.

Civic engagement implies meaningful connections among citizens and among citizens, issues, institutions, and the political system. It implies voice and agency, a feeling of power and effectiveness, with real opportunities to have a say. It implies active participation, with real opportunities to make a difference.

Good communication is key to making and strengthening connections and working relationships. That is why a growing number of civic engagement processes feature some form of public talk or conversation. These processes go by different names—dialogue, deliberation, or public conversation—but the common denominator is face-to-face communication among citizens on issues of common concern.

## A Vision of Democracy at Its Best

Implicit in every civic engagement process is a vision of how democracy and civic life ought to work. For us, the most compelling vision of an ideal democracy is one in which there are ongoing, structured opportunities for everyone to meet as citizens, across different backgrounds and affiliations, and not just as members of a group with similar interests and ideas. In these face-to-face settings, not only does everyone have a voice, but each person also has a way to use that voice in inclusive, diverse, problem-solving conversations that connect directly to action and change.

The Study Circles Resource Center (SCRC), for which we work, was created by the Topsfield Foundation in 1989 to advance deliberative democracy and improve the quality of public life in the United States. Our founder charged us to develop tools that communities can use to involve large numbers of people, from every background and way of life, in face-to-face dialogue and action on critical issues.

In the model SCRC developed to meet this charge, small, diverse groups— *study circles*—meet simultaneously all across a community to address an issue of common concern. In each group, people share their concerns and their personal connections to the issue. They share honestly, listen to each other, form relationships, and build trust. The groups include people of all racial and ethnic backgrounds, men and women, public officials and ordinary citizens, people of all educational backgrounds, and people of all income levels and ages.

These community members determine what is important about the issue facing them. They consider each other's views, find some common ground, and agree to disagree on some things. After meeting several times, they find ways to address the issue; they decide how they want to get involved and make a difference. In addition to meeting in small groups, they also come together, from time to time, as a whole community. That way, the experience of the small group can connect to whole-community processes. People can learn how others are working to make a difference and how their own contribution fits into the larger picture. Some of the people will decide to work together. Some community institutions will decide to work together. Public officials and other community members will engage in a give-and-take of ideas about public policy and find ways to collaborate.

Such opportunities create environments that foster all forms of civic engagement—connecting citizens to each other, to community institutions, to the issues, to policymaking, and to the community as a whole. They also help create a connection between private and public concerns and between community and political concerns. They provide a way to create a strong, diverse community and to make progress on all kinds of social and political issues.

This vision builds on the work of theorists and practitioners who have argued that participatory, citizen-driven democracy is the best avenue for strengthening and reforming civic life. Almost twenty years ago, political scientist Benjamin Barber articulated a compelling version of participatory politics in *Strong Democracy*.[4] In the past several years, civil rights lawyer and law professor Lani Guinier has emphasized the importance of inclusive conversation and deliberation for a participatory democracy that would engage and work for all people. For both Barber and Guinier, face-to-face deliberation provides a remedy to invigorate a democracy that in its current form, does not inspire the participation of its citizens. The remedy comes in creating opportunities for engagement that are meaningful to everyone.[5]

Their assumptions about why people participate in public life mirror what the civic field has begun to understand and articulate about the realities of engagement. People want to be part of community, to have a voice, to connect with all kinds of people, and to make progress on the issues that are important to them. To become engaged, people need to see that their participation will make a difference and that it will be valued. They need opportunities that allow them to make the best use of their skills and time. They need to be invited to participate by those they know and trust.[6]

## The Marriage of Deliberation and Dialogue

This section describes how and why a marriage of dialogue and deliberation is ideally suited to civic efforts that strive to be inclusive, productive, and democratic. The principles we describe here are based on the work of leading thinkers concerning the power and limits of public talk[7] and on more than ten years of observing both the way people talk in civic contexts and how particular types of talk produce different results. Although many of these principles relate to the content and form of the conversation, it is the organizing process that assures a diverse participant group and provides an overarching context for these principles. It is impossible to have a productive public discussion of issues unless everyone's voice and perspective contributes to the search for solutions to public challenges.

The most successful public engagement processes embrace the following principles of talk, dialogue, and deliberation.

1. *Encourage multiple forms of speech and communication to ensure that all kinds of people have a real voice.* Once a diverse group of people comes together in a deliberative dialogue, the process should make it possible for everyone to participate on an equal basis. Political scientist Iris Marion Young believes that deliberative processes are useful to the extent that they promote the use of critical reason (better arguments) instead of raw power. Yet Young also argues that the "norms of deliberation are culturally specific and often operate as forms of power that silence or devalue the speech of some people," noting that predominant "norms of 'articulateness' . . . are culturally specific, and in actual speaking situations . . . exhibiting such speaking styles is a sign of social privilege."[8]

Public engagement processes that are too dependent on the ability of participants to communicate in a single, particular way make it more difficult for everyone to fully participate. To ensure that all kinds of people have a real voice, study circles use a variety of devices, such as ground rules, encouraging reflection on personal experiences, storytelling, brainstorming, and emphasizing the importance of listening.[9]

2. *Make listening as important as speaking.* Most people are not accustomed to having others truly listen to them. Whether we are conversing in everyday settings or participating in a structured process, most of us focus on our own concerns, or prepare our next comment, instead of trying to understand what the other person is really saying. Public opinion analyst Daniel Yankelovich notes that "not being heard is a conditioned response that is constantly reinforced. A typical first reaction to views that oppose your own is to assume that you are not being understood and therefore to restate your own position more insistently, in the hope that the force of your convictions will cause it to register."[10]

A strong emphasis on listening increases the likelihood that more people will participate fully in the discussion. In any group, some people will be more eloquent and comfortable speaking than will others. Processes that promote listening reduce pressure on people who may be reluctant to expose their feelings or ideas before strangers. Good listening also increases the chance that people will truly understand—and even empathize with—each other, thus increasing the odds that they will find common ground for solutions to the public issues being addressed.[11]

Public engagement processes need to go the extra mile to counter our poor listening habits. Study circles encourage respectful, empathetic listening through their use of ground rules and trained peer facilitators. The facilitation style and discussion materials encourage people to ask follow-up questions of their fellow participants to make sure they understand one another. The small size of the group and the time afforded, with a typical sequence of at least four two-hour sessions, reduces the pressure on people to speak before they are ready to do so. And people find it easier to listen when they do not have to jockey for an opportunity to stand in front of large numbers of people and get all their ideas out in one fell swoop.

3. *Connect personal experience with public issues.* The single most effective way to overcome people's initial hesitancy to discuss public issues is to ask them to share their experiences and talk about how the issue at hand affects their daily lives. However, all too often public engagement processes ask people to leap into a discussion of policy options without giving them adequate opportunity to reflect on the relevance of the issue to their own personal experience. If you hope to engage people, you need to "begin where they are" by helping them address public concerns in their own language and on their own terms.[12]

Research conducted by the Harwood Group for the Kettering Foundation looked at the patterns of people's everyday, informal conversations about public issues. The research revealed that most people are not looking for quick answers or decisions on a course of action when they initiate conversations about public issues with family members, friends, co-workers, and neighbors. "Rather, they are striving to better understand what is happening around them and to be understood by others."[13] That is, by engaging in conversation, people are trying to make sense of issues that can be complex and confusing. At the same time, they are strengthening their personal relationships by exploring how others see the issue. Typically, these conversations begin with people venting their frustration about an issue. They also tell personal stories that illustrate how and why they feel the way they do.[14]

At one time or another, all of us have engaged in the type of informal, everyday conversations about public concerns described in the Harwood Group research. Public engagement processes should attempt to take advantage of these habits. For example, study circles focusing on how to build strong neighborhoods begin by asking participants to tell a story about the neighborhoods where they grew up. This is followed by an exercise that asks people to talk about an experience that made them feel connected to their neighborhood.[15] Grounding the discussion in personal experience makes it easier for people who are not accustomed to talking about politics in public to participate fully. It sends the message that everyone's perspective is equally important. This is crucial in situations where some participants may have greater technical knowledge or professional experience than do others. A discussion of personal experience also helps people develop ownership of the issues. While some people may be comfortable discussing concepts or intellectual constructs, others work best when they talk about public issues in concrete terms. Regardless of people's inclinations, beginning a deliberative dialogue by talking about personal experience helps everyone develop greater ownership and understanding of the issue.

4. *Build trust and create a foundation for working relationships.* For deliberative dialogue to lead to meaningful action and change, it must encourage the building of trust and working relationships. Without making an explicit effort to build trust, it is difficult for people to examine publicly the basic assumptions and values that underlie their own views, let alone understand others' perspectives. Moreover, if one of the goals is to help people find ways to create change in a collaborative hands-on way, they need to form working relationships with their fellow participants. As Lani Guinier notes, people are looking for opportunities to "come together to make change, not merely to make friends."[16]

When people consider whether they are willing to work together—to give up or share some of their time, resources, and power—they inevitably ask themselves whether they can trust others to act in good faith. This deep level of trust does not come easily. As noted above, two of the best ways to build trust and mutual understanding are to encourage reflection on personal experience and to emphasize the importance of listening. For some public issues it is important to provide exercises that are intentionally designed to build trust. The initial session of study circles addressing community-police relationships and racial profiling begins by giving mixed groups of residents and police officers the opportunity to discuss questions such as "what did you learn about the police when you were young?" and "if you are a police officer, how do you talk with your family and friends about your job?" This lays the groundwork for a subsequent session on "what do we expect from each other?" where civilians and police officers address questions such as "what makes a good police officer?" and "how does that compare with what makes a good citizen?"[17]

5. *Explore a range of views about the nature of the issue.* Before asking people to make decisions regarding solutions to complex public challenges, deliberative dialogue should help them explore a range of views about the nature of the issue. This is important because, as Richard Harwood (of the Harwood Group) notes, "decision making is not initially a natural part of people's everyday talk about common concerns." Harwood's research makes a strong case that "public engagement techniques often push people in very targeted directions, too often avoiding the natural path that people want to take when it comes to talk. Instead, [we should] think about how to provide people with *opportunities to sort out* what is going on around them."[18]

This process of sorting out what is going on and why it is happening is crucial to people's ability to develop a sense of ownership of public issues. To have this type of deliberative dialogue, participants should use discussion materials that help them explore representative points of view, including those that may be unpopular with some members of the group. Moreover, it is difficult for people to take responsibility for an issue unless the process allows and encourages them to challenge and amend the points of view presented in the materials. Communications theorist John Gastil emphasizes that this ability to "reformulate" or "reframe" an issue is essential if people are to have real power to set the public agenda.[19]

After an initial session in which people get to know one another and establish their personal connection to the issue, study circles encourage participants to explore one or more of the following lines of questioning: (1) How is this issue affecting our community (or region/state/nation)? (2) What is the nature of the problem? (3) What are the root causes of the problem? For example, study circles on immigration do not jump immediately into questions about whether we should allow more or fewer newcomers into the United States. Instead, people begin by talking about the many ways in which increasing numbers of newcomers are affecting schools, race relations, language differences, and competition for jobs. This prepares study circle participants for a subsequent session that asks, "What should we do about immigration and community change?"[20]

6. *Encourage analysis and reasoned argument.* The powerful work that occurs in dialogue—identifying the connections between personal and public concerns, creating mutual understanding, and building relationships based on trust—is necessary for solving complex public problems. But it is not enough. People also need structured opportunities to engage in "judicious argument, critical listening, and earnest decision making."[21] Most political theorists who focus on the importance of public deliberation emphasize the importance of critical thinking and reasoned argument to the creation of sound public policy. David Mathews, president of the Kettering Foundation, has been one of the most vocal and persistent promoters of this concept of public deliberation: "deliberations aren't just discussions to promote better understanding. They are the way we make the decisions that allow us to act together. People are challenged to face the unpleasant costs and consequences of various options and to 'work through' the often volatile emotions that are a part of making public decisions."[22]

The need for reasoned argument raises the question of how much information people need in order to deliberate effectively. Some civic engagement processes stress the importance of exposing participants to large amounts of technical information and other relevant facts. While many theorists and promoters of public deliberation agree that civic engagement processes should provide a baseline of information about issues, they also warn against overwhelming people with too many facts.[23] Richard Harwood emphasizes that civic engagement processes should provide "a sense of coherence about how different pieces of information fit together . . . and not necessarily all available information."[24]

While critical thinking is an essential part of effective engagement on issues, too many civic reformers tend to make this approach the element of political talk that trumps all others. Benjamin Barber notes, "Philosophers and legal theorists have been particularly guilty of overrationalizing talk in their futile quest for a perfectly rational world mediated by perfectly rational forms of speech."[25] Many people are intimidated by processes that place heavy emphasis on absorbing large amounts of facts or on making closely reasoned arguments.[26] Such an approach can make it difficult to bring large and diverse numbers of people into a civic engagement process.

This is one of the most important reasons for combining the best aspects of dialogue and deliberation in a single process. A more comprehensive deliberative dialogue approach provides a place in the process for people who engage public issues in all kinds of ways. As noted above, the first few sessions of a study circle emphasize the dialogue aspects of deliberative dialogue. In most cases, it is not until the penultimate session that a study circle addresses the pros and cons of different proposals for action. By this time, people have become more comfortable with each other and with the issue, making it easier for everyone to have a voice.[27]

7. *Help people develop public judgment and create common ground for action.* Most people who organize and participate in civic engagement processes do so

because they are looking for solutions to public challenges. Social change and action that depends on people working together (as compared to change that is rooted in individual behavior and attitudes) necessitates finding agreement about appropriate courses of action. When diverse groups of people use deliberative dialogue to consider different points of view on public issues, they develop the public judgment and create the common ground that is integral to achieving workable public policy and sustainable community action.

As conceived by Daniel Yankelovich, public judgment is a more mature, considered form of public opinion. "In making a judgment, people take into account the facts as they understand them *and* their personal goals and moral values *and* their sense of what is best for others as well as themselves."[28] Deliberative dialogue is ideal for helping people come to public judgment on complex issues. Using this approach, people can connect their personal experience to an issue, develop mutual understanding, explore values and assumptions, and use reasoned argument and analysis to reach conclusions about the appropriate direction for public policy. Again, according to Yankelovich (referring to how people form a public judgment about capital punishment), "Their social values and personal morality, their interpretation of the meaning of life, and whatever statistics they happen to know about crime rates are all aspects of a single, indivisible judgment."[29] This sort of work is especially important when attempting to create civic engagement processes that inform policymaking at the state and national level.[30]

In addition to developing public judgment that enjoys broad and deep support, civic engagement processes grounded in deliberative dialogue create common ground for action. Political scientist Michael Briand warns that many public processes lead to "least common denominator" solutions in which common ground is "construed as the area of overlap between what you believe or desire and what I believe or desire."[31] This type of agreement can be more of a narrowly defined negotiation than a broad-based foundation for public action. Deliberative dialogue, on the other hand, generates new ideas and civic energy. The marriage of deliberative dialogue with large-scale, inclusive community organizing increases the odds that people will generate new ideas and creative solutions.

Moreover, common ground should not be confused with absolute consensus. When participants reach common ground, they find areas of general agreement. These agreements may lead to some group-supported action ideas and some action ideas that only a portion of the group supports. This is important because participants in a deliberative dialogue feel more at liberty to consider and generate new ideas when they are not obliged to reach total agreement.

8. *Provide a way for people to see themselves as actors and to be actors.* Our everyday public discourse reinforces the idea that real change happens "out there," beyond most people's reach or influence. In part, this reflects the all-too-common disconnects between citizens and elected officials and between

community members and the institutions and resources of the community. It also reflects the difficulty in seeing how individuals' efforts to create change connect to the larger issues or the larger community.

Effective deliberative dialogue processes address this in two ways. First, whole-community organizing creates opportunities for people from various neighborhoods, institutions, and agencies to work through problems, consider solutions, and share a variety of resources to solve them.[32] In essence, the process should bring "us" and "them" together in the conversation, so that the conversation is about "all of us" making a difference in the community. This takes the focus away from "this is what we hope *they* will do."

Second, the content of the deliberative dialogue process is also critical. It helps create a sense of agency for each person by leading participants in a natural progression from analysis of the issue to an exploration of specific action steps. When participants have the chance to consider a range of actions that different actors (such as individuals, small groups, nonprofits, businesses, schools, and government) can take, they are more likely to see that solutions to public problems can come in many and varied ways. They are also more likely to see themselves as actors. When a public conversation ends with analysis of the issue and does not progress to an intentional conversation about action steps, it reinforces the idea that the possibilities for addressing the issue are entirely outside the room.

The final session of a study circle gives participants a chance to follow this natural progression, consider a range of possible actions, and decide which action steps they see as most important. Then they present those action priorities at a large-group meeting (often referred to as an *action forum*) that gives all the small groups a chance to pool their ideas and move forward on a range of actions. It is also important to keep the results of the deliberative dialogue process in the public eye. This helps people see the value of their participation.[33] Some communities have developed benchmarks for change to help participants and the larger community measure the progress they are making. This recognition of change encourages sustained efforts and also inspires broader participation.

We have found that the marriage of community organizing to deliberative dialogue is essential for bringing this principle to life. While it is possible for people in small-scale engagement processes to consider possible action steps, a diverse, large-scale process opens up many more avenues for action that can address institutional, community-wide, and policy dimensions of issues.[34]

9. *Connect to government, policymaking, and governance.* A common practice in public talk processes is to ask participants to report the results of their deliberation to elected officials. Yet if the process does not include a way to establish trust and mutuality between citizens and government, it will fall short of helping them work together more effectively. Some engagement processes include ways to capture themes and convey them to public officials. Identifying areas of common ground among members of the public can be especially

useful to legislators who are looking for ways to reframe adversarial public policy debates. But the more effective input processes go one step further: they involve the policymakers as participants on an equal basis in the dialogue.

Democratic conversation between citizens and government has always been central to the ideal (if not practice) of democracy. A current-day example is Benjamin Barber's call for "horizontal conversations among citizens rather than the more usual vertical conversation typical of communication between citizens and elites."[35] This type of process makes it more likely that the input will be meaningful to officials, and thus acted on. It creates a context of reciprocity and relationship building that makes for a nonthreatening way for public officials to reevaluate their own perspectives on policy issues, and for citizens to have their voices heard in a more meaningful way. In Oklahoma, the League of Women Voters and several other organizations organized a statewide study circle program on criminal justice and corrections. The study circles occurred in thirteen communities across the state and included state legislators. The involvement of legislators in the deliberative dialogue helped break a long-standing deadlock on corrections policy and helped create a radical revision of the criminal justice system.[36]

The full engagement of citizens goes beyond problem solving and input to shared governance. This can happen when the process involves public officials from the outset, as full partners in the organizing process and in the dialogue, with a commitment to sharing decision making. This differs significantly from mere input. First, it provides a way for citizens and officials to work together in the day-to-day activities and decisions of governing, not just when there is a crisis or a deadlock. Second, it provides ways to envision a different practice of politics.

Political scientist Archon Fung and sociologist Erik Olin Wright have examined the use of deliberative processes that include residents and public officials in solving specific, tangible problems. They see what they call "empowered deliberative democracy" as leading to better outcomes than those that would emerge in more typical top-down situations, and to increased and more diverse citizen participation.[37] In another example, a community-wide study circle program in Decatur, Georgia, included the city commission as part of the organizing process from the very beginning. The circles produced over 400 recommendations for a range of community problems, many of which were acted on by city government. In a research study prepared for the Kettering Foundation, John Gastil and Todd Kelshaw noted that the Decatur study circle process created what they termed "collaborative deliberation," which occurs "when citizen leaders and policymakers are both familiar with the practice of deliberation, and they co-create a public space for talking about the public's problems." They hypothesized that of all the kinds of processes for bringing together citizens and officeholders, this "collaborative form of deliberation may be the most fruitful in the long run because we suspect that it tends to transform the way citizens and officeholders practice politics."[38]

10. *Create ongoing processes, not isolated events.* It seems inconceivable that any public engagement process could meet ambitious goals in a single two- or three-hour session. Nevertheless, organizers of many public engagement processes often ask people to do just that. When SCRC first began advising communities on how to organize deliberative dialogue, we encouraged local organizers of study circles to plan one-time events. We did this because a single event takes less work, time, and expense to organize than does a series of meetings. Local organizers also worried that most people would not commit to more than one meeting.

Our approach changed in 1993 when study circle organizers began calling for a more comprehensive approach to address the challenges of racism and race relations. They told us that their communities could not make significant progress on difficult public issues such as racism and race relations, education, or crime in a single, brief meeting. People who wanted to learn a little more about an issue might be content with meeting once, but those who were interested in effecting meaningful change were prepared to commit to a more thorough process. People found it difficult to move toward solutions until they had experienced many of the dynamics inherent in deliberative dialogue described here.

There is, of course, a trade-off between the time commitment a process calls for and the number of people who will participate. Lack of time is a major barrier to participation in any civic activity.[39] People are less likely to commit to taking part in long, drawn-out processes. Ideally, the time should be divided into at least three or four separate meetings over a period of several weeks. This format feels natural to participants because it mirrors the way people approach public issues in informal settings. It allows time for reflection. As Richard Harwood notes, in their everyday conversations, "people reach closure on their concerns as talk evolves over time."[40] Between weekly sessions, study circles encourage participants to talk informally about the issue with friends, family members, co-workers and others (keeping confidential the identity of who said what within the study circle), and to pay attention to how the issue is playing out in the news and in their community. A broader range of insights is thus introduced to the circle and throughout the community.

## The Marriage of Community Organizing and Deliberative Dialogue

Many public talk processes concentrate on the quality of the conversation itself, but few have concentrated on finding cost-effective and sustainable ways to bring large numbers of people to the table, or have aspired to explicitly connect the talk to change in the larger community. Both of these aims are critical if a deliberative dialogue process is to lead to meaningful civic engagement. Civic engagement processes (in particular, those that rely on some form of public talk) must address two essential questions: who should be in the conversation and how will the talk connect to action and change? Our answers to these questions are based on what we have learned from study circle organizers and participants in hundreds of communities across the United States.

The short answer to the question of *who* should be in the conversation is everyone. This comes directly from a vision of participatory democracy, in which no one's voice can take the place of—or fully represent—someone else's voice. Neither can anyone experience engagement on behalf of someone else. The fulfillment and impact that come from making connections with other community members and the community as a whole cannot be delegated or experienced vicariously. This answer also proceeds from the reality of what it takes to find lasting solutions to public problems—and to implement them. For most public issues, progress can be made only when large numbers of ordinary people bring their voices, including their ideas, their passions, and their energy, to addressing them.

Although, admittedly, no one has (yet) literally engaged an entire community, many community coalitions have involved hundreds and sometimes thousands of people from every background and way of life. Some have succeeded in building an infrastructure for engagement that continues to enlarge and diversify the circle of participation. In working with these groups, we have observed what works best in creating large-scale engagement processes, and we have documented and disseminated information about those practices.[41] While nothing this complex can be condensed into an off-the-shelf model, we have developed principles, guidelines, questions, and templates for each stage of organizing, all of which we are continuously refining.[42]

Those within the civic field increasingly recognize that individuals are more likely to take part in public life when they are recruited by people whom they know and trust.[43] It follows that successful large-scale civic engagement processes require strong, diverse coalitions of community groups and individuals dedicated to bringing community members to the table for meaningful engagement. No single organization or institution acting on its own can mobilize the whole community.

Effective recruitment is enhanced when the galvanizing issue is of concern to all kinds of people and draws the participation and sponsorship of a broad array of community institutions and individuals. About half of all communities with which we work have begun a large-scale engagement process around the issue of racism and race relations. Because racial divides and inequities underlie so many other public issues, and because effective multiracial civic networks are absent in most communities, starting with this issue helps lay the groundwork for civic engagement on a whole range of issues.[44] Education reform, criminal corrections, neighborhood issues, and community police relationships are among the other issues that communities have addressed.

The need to engage the whole community leads directly to the question: how will the talk connect to action and change? We have found that only by making explicit connections among deliberative dialogue, action, and change is it possible to mobilize large numbers of people. When people call us to ask about study circles, most are not calling to say that they want to improve public life or enhance deliberative democracy. They are calling because they want to engage people in their community around solving or addressing a particular issue. Very few people will take the time to get engaged in a structured public conversation or any other engagement process unless they believe there is a strong possibility that their efforts will lead to tangible results. Without intentional connection to change, engagement loses its meaning.

Table 1 provides a framework for thinking about how community-wide deliberative dialogue leads to many different forms of action and change.

We have found that a process of deliberative dialogue that aspires to engage the whole community must do the following: provide opportunities to consider various kinds of action and change; provide ways for people to see themselves as actors in the community; make clear (from the outset of organizing) that the community-wide dialogue is aimed at action and change; provide explicit connections to change processes and institutions; validate action and change at individual, group, institutional, and whole-community levels; and give people a wide variety of possibilities for involvement so that they can become engaged in change processes as their interest and time allow.

## Conclusion

The movement to strengthen democracy and civic life is searching for ways to expand and deepen civic engagement. A growing number of civic engagement processes include some form of public talk. In this article we have described what we have learned about public talk that is rooted in a vision of strong, participatory democracy. Our response to the key question of "Who should be in the conversation?" is *everyone*. That answer (and our literal, if ultimate, goal) has translated into a search for processes and principles that will bring large numbers of people into a diverse, democratic conversation that is an ongoing part of public life. To welcome everyone, such a conversation must be intentionally linked to all kinds and levels of action and change.

We maintain that two unique marriages are essential to creating public talk that aims to engage the whole community. First, dialogue and deliberation as usually understood need to be combined. This *deliberative dialogue* creates a more holistic form of communication that acknowledges the importance of building community connections and of collective action and shared work. Second, community organizing and deliberative dialogue must be combined in an effort to bring everyone to the table and to create a true public context for public conversation.

We believe that deliberative dialogue that engages the whole community can further the goals of the larger civic movement and hope that this article will spark a conversation among practitioners and theorists about the kind of talk that democracy needs. In concert with e.ThePeople, an Internet-based

**Table 1. Action and Change in Study Circle Programs**

| Kind of Change | How Does It Happen? | Example |
|---|---|---|
| Changes in individual behavior and attitudes | Better understanding of the issues and of one another inspires people to "make a difference." | A participant in a community-wide program on racism decides never again to let racist remarks go by without a comment. |
| New relationships and networks | Trust and understanding develop between participants in the dialogue. | Following study circles on community-police relationships, young people and police officers hold weekly meetings. |
| New working collaborations | Individuals and organizations develop new relationships and new ideas for solutions. | After study circles on neighborhood issues, residents, police officers, and mental health advocates create an emergency team to help mentally ill people who wander the streets. |
| Institutional changes | Leaders and members of an institution gain new insights in study circles that lead to changes within the institution and in the larger community. | After doing study circles on race, leaders of several banks work with others to improve banking services to communities of color. |
| Changes in public policy | Public officials help organize study circles and pledge to work with citizens to implement action ideas.<br>or<br>Public officials take part in the organizing *and* dialogue and gain new insights that have an impact on their policymaking.<br>or | Following study circles on education, participants develop a plan to close the gap in achievement between the races. The school board—a leading organizer of the circles—funds the plan and helps carry it out.<br><br>After participating in study circles, a school superintendent creates |

*(continued)*

**Table 1. (continued)**

| Kind of Change | How Does It Happen? | Example |
|---|---|---|
|  | Information from the study circles is collected and reported to decision makers. | new policies to involve parents in the district's schools. |
|  |  | A report from study circles on growth and sprawl is turned over to the planning board, which uses this information to help shape the town's strategic plan. |
| Changes in community dynamics | Many hundreds of people take part in study circles. Once there is a "critical mass" of people who have a new understanding of issues and of one another, their capacity for community work increases. | Study circles on race relations happen in a community over years. In all kinds of settings, public meetings begin to operate according to study circle principles. People learn to work together across differences and feel a stronger sense of community. |
| Changes in a community's public life | Once people see the benefits to action of large-scale dialogue, they make it an ongoing part of how their community works. | After a round of study circles on education, the school district decides to use study circles routinely to involve citizens in creating and implementing its annual school-improvement plan. |

public forum operated by the Democracy Project, SCRC will be hosting a Democratic Renewal eConference to explore further ways of strengthening democracy through civic engagement. More information can be found on the Web site www.studycircles.org.

## Notes

1. Yankelovich, D. *The Magic of Dialogue: Transforming Conflict into Cooperation.* New York: Simon & Schuster, 1999, provides a very useful overview of the many uses of dialogue.

2. Mathews, D. "Dialogue and Deliberation: 'Meaning Making' Is Essential to Decision Making." *Connections,* Dec. 1998, 9(2), pp. 24–27.

3. We believe that when you combine these two marriages, it provides a practical set of solutions that address some of the dilemmas posed in Lynn Sanders' cogent critique of deliberation. She notes that deliberation as it is often idealized or practiced excludes many voices and perspectives. See Sanders, L. M. "Against Deliberation." *Political Theory,* 1997, *25,* 347–376.

4. Barber, B. *Strong Democracy: Participatory Politics for a New Age.* Berkeley: University of California Press, 1984. In *A Place for Us: How to Make Society Civil and Democracy Strong.* New York: Hill and Wang, 1998, Barber clarifies notions of civil society.

5. Guinier, L. *Lift Every Voice: Turning a Civil Rights Setback into a New Vision of Social Justice.* New York: Simon & Schuster, 1998. See also Guinier, L. "What Is Democracy?" Speech to the Funders' Committee on Citizen Participation, Aug. 1997. Others who have articulated this vision of democracy are Boyte, H. C., and Kari, N. N. *Building America: The Democratic Promise of Public Work.* Philadelphia: Temple University Press, 1996; Shumer, S. M., and Pitkin, H. F. "On Participation." *Democracy,* Fall 1982, 2(4), 43–54; Wiebe, R. H. *Self Rule: A Cultural History of American Democracy.* Chicago: University of Chicago Press, 1995, especially pp. 251–252; Young, I. M. "Communication and the Other: Beyond Deliberative Democracy." In S. Behabib (ed.), *Democracy and Difference.* Princeton: Princeton University Press, 1996, pp. 120–135.

6. In 1999, the League of Women Voters of the United States commissioned Lake Snell Perry & Associates and The Tarrance Group to conduct a multiphase project on civic participation. The report on the project, based on one-on-one interviews with local activists, small-group interviews with citizens in four cities around the country, and a national survey, is available at www.lwv.org/elibrary/pub/cp_survey/cp_1.html. See also Michael X. Delli Carpini's comments in "The State of the Movement." *National Civic Review: Making Citizen Democracy Work,* Summer 2000, 89(2), 122–126.

7. Some of the sources we found particularly helpful in considering the key elements of deliberative democratic dialogue that lead to action and change are Barber (1984), pp. 173–198; Gastil, J. *By Popular Demand: Revitalizing Representative Democracy Through Deliberative Elections.* Berkeley: University of California Press, 2000; Harwood, R., Perry, M., and Schmitt, W. *Meaningful Chaos: How People Form Relationships with Public Concerns.* Dayton: Kettering Foundation, 1993; Harwood, R., Scully, P., and Dennis, K. *Will Any Kind of Talk Do? Moving from Personal Concerns to Public Life.* Dayton: Kettering Foundation and The Harwood Group, 1996; Mathews, D. *Politics for People: Finding a Responsible Public Voice.* Urbana: University of Illinois Press, 1994; Mathews, D., and McAfee, N. *Making Choices Together: The Power of Public Deliberation.* Dayton: Kettering Foundation, 2000; Yankelovich (1999); and Young (1996).

8. Young (1996), pp. 123–124.

9. Young (1996), p. 129, calls for a "communicative democracy" that, in addition to critical argument, values "greeting, rhetoric, and storytelling." She also makes a case for "nonlinguistic gestures that bring people together warmly . . . smiles, handshakes, hugs, the giving and taking of food and drink."

10. Yankelovich (1999), p. 136.

11. Yankelovich (1999), pp. 43–44, and Barber (1984), pp. 175–176, emphasize the importance of empathetic listening.

12. Eliasoph, N. *Avoiding Politics: How Americans Produce Apathy in Everyday Life.* Cambridge: Cambridge University Press, 1998, pp. 10, 231, describes the extreme difficulty that people have creating "contexts for political conversation in everyday life." She also makes the case that well-designed processes and lines of questioning make it possible for hitherto inactive citizens to engage in meaningful political discussion.

13. Harwood, Scully, and Dennis (1996), p. 9.

14. Harwood, Scully, and Dennis (1996), p. 4.

15. Leighninger, M., Flavin-McDonald, C., and Ghandour, R. *Building Strong Neighborhoods: A Study Circle Guide for Public Dialogue and Community Problem Solving.* Pomfret, Conn.: Topsfield Foundation, 1998.

16. Guinier (1998), p. 307.

17. Archie, M., and Terry, H. D. *Protecting Communities, Serving the Public: Police and Residents Building Relationships to Work Together.* Pomfret, Conn.: Topsfield Foundation, 2000.

18. Harwood, Scully, and Dennis (1996), p. 6. Emphasis in the original.

19. Gastil, J. *Democracy in Small Groups: Participation, Decision Making & Communication.* Philadelphia: New Society, 1993, p. 27.

20. Scully, P., and Leighninger, M. *Changing Faces, Changing Communities: Immigration & Race, Jobs, Schools, and Language Differences* (2nd ed.). Pomfret, Conn.: Topsfield Foundation, 1998.

21. Gastil (2000), p. 22.

22. Mathews and McAfee (2000), p. 4.

23. Yankelovich (1999), p. 24, discounts the importance of giving people technical information. "The premise that the health of our democracy depends on a well-informed public is one of those unexamined pieties that professionals mouth without ever observing close-up how people really make the judgments on which our society does depend."

24. Harwood, Perry, and Schmitt (1993), p. 44.

25. Barber (1984), p. 176.

26. Harwood, Scully, and Dennis (1996), pp. 17–18.

27. Yankelovich (1999), p. 57, notes that "[e]ven when the sole purpose of a dialogue is to reach a decision, the dialogue part of the process should precede the decision-making part."

28. Yankelovich (1999), p. 179.

29. Yankelovich (1999), p. 179.

30. See Fishkin, J. S. *Democracy and Deliberation: New Directions for Democratic Reform.* New Haven: Yale University Press, 1991; Levine, P. *The New Progressive Era: Toward a Fair and Deliberative Democracy.* Lanham, Md.: Rowman & Littlefield, 2000; Lukensmeyer, C., and Goldman, J. P. *A National Townhall: Bringing Citizens Together Through Interactive Video Teleconferencing.* Washington, D.C.: The Tides Center/Americans Discuss Social Security, 1999; The Jefferson Center. *The Citizen Jury: Effective Public Participation.* Minneapolis: Jefferson Center for New Democratic Processes, 1999.

31. Briand, M. *Practical Politics: Five Principles for a Community That Works.* Urbana: University of Illinois Press, 1999, pp. 222–223, n. 2.

32. *Study Circles; Sharing Our Experiences: Engaging Residents in Family Strengthening Efforts: Des Moines, Indianapolis, and Seattle.* A report of the Technical Assistance Resource Center for the Making Connections Initiative of the Annie E. Casey Foundation, Aug. 2000.

33. Flavin-McDonald, C. *Study Circles on Racism & Race Relations: Year 1, 1997: A Report on the Focus Groups.* Pomfret, Conn.: Study Circles Resource Center/YWCA of New Castle County, 1998.

34. *Toward Competent Communities: Best Practices for Producing Community-Wide Study Circles.* Lexington, Mass.: Roberts & Kay, 2000, chap. 9.

35. Barber (1998), p. 85.

36. "Balancing Justice in Oklahoma." *Focus on Study Circles,* Winter 1997, 8(1). See also Mutchler, S. E., and Pan, D. T. *Calling the Roll: Study Circles for Better Schools: Policy Research Report.* Austin: Southwest Educational Development Laboratory, Sept. 2000. Statewide study circle programs in Oklahoma and Arkansas involved state legislators as part of the deliberative dialogue. Interviews with the legislators revealed that many benefited from increased access to information; a reality check on policy directions; a way to reevaluate and change their perspectives; a stronger commitment to ongoing work with the public, and a stronger commitment toward policy to support public education.

37. See Fung, A., and Wright, E. O. "Deepening Democracy: Innovations in Empowered Participatory Governance." *Politics and Society,* Mar. 2001, 29(1). Fung and Wright also consider critiques and limits of deliberative democracy.

38. Gastil, J., and Kelshaw, T. "Public Meetings: A Sampler of Deliberative Forums That Bring Officeholders and Citizens Together." Draft report prepared for the Kettering Foundation, May 2000; for other examples and analysis, see Leighninger, M. "Shared Governance." *Public Organization Review* (forthcoming).

39. See note 5.

40. Harwood, Scully, and Dennis (1996), p. 25. This dynamic holds true for most public issues. Commenting on political scientist James Fishkin's 1996 National Issues Convention, Daniel Yankelovich (1999, p. 200, n. 4) argues that the theory of deliberation guiding these types of events is "too rationalistic and short term," and notes that "People rarely change strongly held positions after a few hours of calm, reasonable conversation."

41. Elliott, V., Houlé, K., Kay, S., Nagda, B., and Roberts, R. *What Works: Study Circles in the Real World.* Lexington, Mass.: Roberts & Kay, 2000.

42. Campbell, S. vL., Malick, A., and McCoy, M. L. *Organizing Community-Wide Dialogue for Action and Change.* Pomfret, Conn.: Topsfield Foundation, 2001. [www.studycircles.org/pages/hap.html].

43. In essence, this model is trying to create the new associational forms that Theda Skocpol has envisioned. Skocpol, T. "Advocates Without Members: The Recent Transformation of American Civic Life." In T. Skocpol and M. P. Fiorina (eds.), *Civic Engagement in American Democracy.* Washington, D.C.: Brookings Institution Press, 1999, pp. 461–509.

44. This is demonstrated in *Toward Competent Communities* (2000), [www.studycircles.org/pages/best.html].

*Martha L. McCoy is executive vice president of the Topsfield Foundation and executive director of the Study Circles Resource Center.*

*Patrick L. Scully is vice president of the Topsfield Foundation and deputy director of the Study Circles Resource Center.*

# Enlisting Citizens: Building Political Legitimacy

*Matt Leighninger*

In the first few months of 2002, the Bush administration launched several major initiatives aimed at restoring the health of civic life in the United States. These new ventures, which include the USA Freedom Corps and the Citizen Corps, are intended to increase volunteerism and community service and promote a more active concept of citizenship. The choice of the term corps recalls earlier undertakings such as the Civilian Conservation Corps and the Peace Corps. Like these programs, the president's new initiatives are federally orchestrated efforts to build and strengthen communities. Yet recent examples of grassroots organizing demonstrate a different vision for mobilizing a citizenry to greater involvement.

At the local level across the country, a burgeoning civic participation movement is much less centralized and uniform than the efforts inaugurated by the Bush administration. The leadership of these diverse projects ranges from community activists to school board members, human relations commissioners, and public officials, among others. Though their programs reflect the same democratic principles and use many of the same strategies, each effort is locally directed and specific to the situation in that community.

Recent projects in Oklahoma, Minnesota, and New York evince a powerful new tactic deployed by the democratic organizers who orchestrated them: the ability to mobilize citizens by confirming their political legitimacy and providing them with a sense of political efficacy. Political legitimacy recognizes that citizens have public privileges and responsibilities. Political efficacy means that their opinions and actions carry weight with public officials and fellow citizens. The projects discussed here involved thousands of people, enlisted hundreds of volunteers, and led to policy changes at the state and local levels, but their most important contribution may have been that citizens gained the sense that they matter. It is to be hoped this realization will lead them to embrace the active and comprehensive vision of citizenship that the Bush administration is trying to stimulate through its recent initiatives.

## Democratic Organizing and Political Efficacy

Deliberative forums, such as those organized by the Study Circles Resource Center (SCRC) (see the article in this issue by McCoy and Scully, "Deliberative Dialogue to Expand Civic Engagement," for a description of study circles), and other democratic organizing projects convene groups of people to discuss issues and to participate in making public decisions. The projects in Oklahoma, Minnesota, and New York described here were carefully designed to reinforce participants' sense of legitimacy and enhance their input on decision making. The organizers worked with local newspapers, featured state legislators and other public officials, gave specific titles to citizens in the program, supplied participants with officially approved "fact books," released carefully assembled reports, and employed pomp and circumstance at every turn.

All three programs were spearheaded by state chapters of the League of Women Voters. It is also interesting that two of the projects focused on the justice system and the third addressed immigration issues. Both topics deal with the relationship between the community and the individual and force us to examine our expectations for citizens. What kind of message about roles and responsibilities should the community give to newcomers who want to join it? What should we ask of ex-offenders who want to rejoin it?

*Balancing Justice in Oklahoma.* In 1996, Oklahoma's obsession with criminal justice could be captured in one image: Timothy McVeigh, wearing an orange bulletproof suit and handcuffs, being led to a police vehicle through a crowd of shouting people. The Oklahoma City bomber had become a symbol for an intensely emotional, multifaceted issue. Carol Scott, then president of the League of Women Voters in Oklahoma, and Trish Frazier, the executive director of the organization, realized that the political system was not helping Oklahomans address one of the most important issues they faced. In 1995, Oklahoma had the third-highest incarceration rate in the country; during the following fiscal year, it spent $247 million of a relatively small state budget on corrections.

Over the years, the League had put the corrections issue higher and higher on its legislative agenda. But in the 1995 and 1996 sessions of the state legislature, proposals for truth in sentencing and community corrections failed amid raucous debate. Even the most basic facts were in dispute; for example, corrections and law enforcement officials were unable to agree on how to count the offenders who were in the system. To help avoid such train wrecks in the future, Scott and Frazier took an unusual step. Rather than lobbying the legislature on a new reform bill, they decided to involve hundreds of citizens in study circles to discuss priorities for the criminal justice system. The deliberations from these meetings would be compiled into a single report that would then be given to the legislature. Scott and Frazier embarked on a statewide study circle program, striving to involve one thousand people in one hundred study circles in communities all over Oklahoma.

The League enlisted the help of other organizations at the state and local levels including the Oklahoma Conference of Churches, the Oklahoma Academy for State Goals, and the Citizen's League of Central Oklahoma as well as parent-teacher associations, chambers of commerce, churches, community action groups, court systems, police and sheriff's departments, corrections employee unions, victims' groups, inmate support groups, colleges and universities, and local government officials.

As a basis for the discussions, each study circle used a guide called *Balancing Justice: Setting Citizen Priorities for the Corrections System.* The guide was designed to help citizens work through what the goals of the criminal justice system ought to be, consider the current corrections dilemma, and talk about what they could do to make changes. In the fall of 1996, the Balancing Justice study circles got under way. Over the next six months, 972 people participated in thirteen communities, ranging from Tulsa and Oklahoma City to small towns throughout the state.

**Spreading a Sense of Legitimacy.** One of the most effective ways to mobilize citizens is to show them that they are part of something larger than themselves. The Oklahoma plan, which was used later in Minnesota and New York, successfully accomplished this by using the following critical components.

*Kickoff to Announce and Officially Begin the Program.* Frazier organized a kickoff event in Oklahoma City to inaugurate Balancing Justice at the state level, and she encouraged the local organizers to hold their own kickoffs. Kickoffs typically included high-profile speakers, an explanation of the program, and testimonials from people who participated in pilot study circles. By providing an official ceremony to launch the program, organizers were able to convey the expectation that the study circles would be a meaningful political activity through which citizen voices would be heard.

*The Presence of Public Officials.* Public officials, including legislators, judges, sheriffs, and mayors (and even some candidates running for elected office) attended many of the kickoffs and study circles. Several participants remarked that this was the first time they had been able to have a meaningful conversation with an elected official or candidate. The active participation of public officials and the seriousness with which they listened to citizen ideas and concerns gave the other participants a chance to be part of the policy-making process.

*Meetings Open to a Range of People and Views.* The fact that people of many different backgrounds and political inclinations attended the Balancing Justice meetings gave these meetings more legitimacy. The organizers who assembled the report of the groups that met in Weatherford, Oklahoma, wrote: "Those involved included lawyers, law enforcement officers, public service agencies, church leaders, city officials and administrators, private business people, university students/staff/faculty, retired persons, candidates for elected offices, homemakers (male and female), and more. There were victims, offenders, and observers of the criminal justice system. Every political persuasion seemed included: Democrats, Republicans, Independents, conservatives, moderates, and liberals. In short, citizens."

*A Structured and Information-Intensive Process.* With assistance from SCRC, Scott and Frazier trained local facilitators, advised local organizers about setting up their circles, and provided them with copies of the *Balancing Justice* guide. To give the study circle participants a greater grounding in the issue, the League also created a nonpartisan fact book of information and statistics about the criminal justice system. In delving into the complexities of the criminal justice system, citizens developed a greater understanding of the policymaking process.

*Participation of the League.* Long before the program began, the League's tradition of studying policy decisions carefully and intensively had given the organization a great deal of political legitimacy. Just as League-sponsored candidate debates lend an air of legitimacy to political campaigns, the imprimatur of the Oklahoma League gave Balancing Justice a greater degree of credibility.

**Success in Surprising Ways.** In their discussions, Balancing Justice participants identified two major goals for the corrections system: incapacitation of violent offenders and rehabilitation of all offenders. They advocated two policy ideas to realize these goals: truth in sentencing and community-based corrections. These ideas turned out to be the main components of the legislation.

Prior to the release of the final report from the Balancing Justice project, the Oklahoma House passed House Bill 1213, one of the most radical revisions of the criminal justice system in the history of the state. The bill passed unexpectedly early, on its first day out of committee. By the time it passed the Senate the next day, HB1213 had been approved by the astonishing combined vote of 140 to 2.

The League had expected that the final report would make the most impact. "As it turned out, three factors were far more important than the report," said Tony Hutchison, a legislative aide. "First, a lot of legislators attended the study circles. Second, other public officials—people legislators talk to about policy, like judges and sheriffs—attended the circles. Third, there was good media coverage for the meetings, so without attending a session you could pick up a newspaper the next day and find out what people's main conclusions had been."

In addition to upholding the main recommendations of Balancing Justice, the Oklahoma legislature provided latitude for greater citizen involvement in corrections policy. HB 1213 gave local governments the responsibility for dealing with many low-level offenders. The bill included a mandate for community input, requiring that community boards make decisions about local implementation. This democratic sentiment mirrored some of the statements made by study circle participants in their reports. "We would like for the Balancing Justice circles to be effective 'change agents,' and help to set policies that are balanced. Our group and others like us, as concerned citizens taking time to work on these things, should have a say," an Oklahoma City study circle reported.

The controversies over state-level legislation had drawn many citizens to the circles, but once they began examining the issue, many study circle participants discovered that they could make a difference in their own backyards. At the local level, Balancing Justice led eventually to drug courts, teen courts, mentoring programs for inmates and parolees, church outreach programs for former offenders, and job-training partnerships between local businesses and corrections facilities.

At the beginning, Scott and Frazier thought of democratic organizing primarily as an exercise in citizen education. "However, the program went beyond citizen education," says Scott, "to a point of citizen ownership and collaboration with local and state policy makers." Participants did not want just to recommend solutions to their state's corrections crisis; many of them were ready and willing to be part of those solutions.

Though Balancing Justice in Oklahoma received little attention in the national news media, it got some notice among the growing circle of people interested in invigorating civic life in America. In the state League of Women Voters offices in Minnesota and New York, it inspired the creation of two similarly ambitious programs.

***Changing Faces, Changing Communities in Minnesota.*** Minnesota has long been regarded as a predominantly liberal, Lutheran state with a population of largely Scandinavian origin. But over the last ten years, thousands of immigrants from all over the world have moved to Minnesota, and the state's foreign-born population is believed to have grown by 50 percent. Minnesota now has the largest population of Somali immigrants in the United States, and nearly 17,000 Hmong refugees have arrived from refugee camps in Laos. Each summer between 15,000 and 20,000 Mexican migrant farm workers find work in the state.

These demographic shifts are even more apparent in the smaller cities and towns than in the big cities. In Worthington, for instance, a town of 10,260 people, more than fifty languages are spoken in the public schools. In Pelican Rapids, formerly a tourist town of 1,900 residents, twenty-four languages are spoken in the schools. The changes brought by immigration have had an enormous impact on the economic and cultural life of communities all over the state.

Nancy Kari and Harry Boyte had watched these shifts closely. Kari was a co-founder of the Jane Addams School for Democracy, a community-based education and social action initiative in St. Paul. Boyte is a co-director of the Center for Democracy and Citizenship at the University of Minnesota. The pair had been involved in community circles at the Jane Addams School with Hmong and Hispanic residents, college students, and longtime residents.

When Kari and Boyte heard about Balancing Justice in Oklahoma, they recognized that some of the same principles they had seen working in the Jane

Addams circles were being applied in the Oklahoma project on a much larger geographical scale. They approached the office of the League of Women Voters with the idea of a statewide program on immigration. Judy Duffy, president of the League in Minnesota, was intrigued, and the seeds were sown for Changing Faces, Changing Communities: Immigration in Minnesota. To provide a framework for the sessions, the League adapted *Changing Faces, Changing Communities,* a study circle guide published by SCRC, and added information specific to Minnesota. The new guide included a session, written by Kari and Boyte, which helped participants to consider "what it means to be an American in the current age of immigration."

The League attracted funding from several state foundations for the project and followed the formula for political legitimacy established in Oklahoma, advising local coordinators to hold kickoffs, involve public officials, and recruit a range of people and views. They ended up with seventeen sites, from the Twin Cities and their suburbs to little Pelican Rapids. In February 2000, seventy community circles got under way, involving 961 people.

***Building a Broader Community.*** Many of the immediate local outcomes of Changing Faces, Changing Communities were ethnic festivals and diversity celebrations. In at least one instance, the circles helped the members of an immigrant group recapture a part of their culture they had lost: a Somali man in Marshall connected with a local farmer who was willing to sell goats to the Somali community. The goats are slaughtered as part of a religious ceremony, and the meat is distributed to Somali families.

Some of the other action ideas were aimed at helping recent immigrants find their voices politically and equipping them to succeed economically. In Edina, the school district hired an additional social worker to assess the needs of immigrant families and connect them with human services programs. A hospital in Marshall has started a program in which Somali women are taught to sew and are given job opportunities to pursue this skill. In Winona, a local technical college agreed to help immigrants learn keyboarding skills. A number of communities have expanded access to ESL classes. Participants in several communities proposed welcome centers or multicultural resource centers. These centers were envisioned as locations where immigrants could organize, socialize, and get access to public services, as well as places for immigrants and longtime residents to meet and interact. At least one, in Pelican Rapids, has been built.

Participants in Pelican Rapids worried that the recent immigrants in their community would be undercounted in the 2000 census, resulting in insufficient state and federal funding for social services. They took the lead in training the census takers in reaching out to immigrant communities, and they conducted a media campaign to encourage immigrants to step forward. When the count was taken, "the census report showed a dramatic increase in population," said Connie Payson, a social worker in Pelican Rapids. "I believe that if we hadn't pushed for a strong census initiative after the circles, we might have missed most of our minority population."

**This *Is What It Means to Be a Citizen*.**  Changing Faces, Changing Communities affected people's thinking about the duties, powers, and privileges of citizenship. Native Minnesotans discovered a more active kind of citizenship than they had known before. In the light of this new experience, they began rethinking their political assumptions. "It's an eye-opening topic," said a participant in Mankato. "Is it citizen in name only, or do we really exercise our responsibility?" The program also gave many of the newer Minnesotans their first meaningful opportunity to participate in public life. They were empowered by an environment where they could share their ideas, feel that they were heard, and find allies with whom they could work. Though some of these newer immigrants had taken the U.S. citizenship test, been sworn in as citizens, and voted, their discussions in the circles may have been their first substantive political experience in this country.

The action forum for the state, which was held in St. Paul, attracted a large and enthusiastic crowd. Each community was given a chance to report on the findings of its circles. "Two things struck me about the forum," Kari said. "First, citizens took those community reports very seriously, and were adamant about the need to move forward on the issue. Second, on several occasions I heard people look around at their fellow attendees and say, '*This* is what it means to be a citizen.' Before this project, they might not have been able to describe what citizenship meant to them, but at the action forum it was clear that they knew it when they saw it."

At its inception, Changing Faces, Changing Communities appeared to promise more of an affirmation of what Minnesota was than a glimpse of what it could be. But in the course of the program, Minnesotans saw that their state was already more complicated and diverse than it appeared. By emphasizing citizens' political legitimacy, the organizers helped participants clarify their political vision. Both the relative newcomers and the longtime residents saw more clearly what a citizen was and what citizenship could be.

**Balancing Justice in New York.**  Balancing Justice in New York (BJNY) first took shape at a meeting of ten people at a church in Albany in 1998. Paddy Lane, a longtime activist on criminal justice issues, brought the group together to float the idea of a program similar to the one in Oklahoma. As an activist, Paddy knew from hard-earned experience what it was like to promote change from the outside. "I felt I'd been able to make a difference in some ways, through efforts like the Alternatives to Violence Project. But I was tired of banging my head against the wall, trying to change a system that didn't want to change. Balancing Justice in Oklahoma appealed to me because it seemed like a way to get a lot of people—including some who worked in the system or were caught up in the system—to see the bigger picture and do something about it." She approached the New York League of Women Voters' executive director, Lee Serravillo, and out of their conversations and the discussions in the Albany church, BJNY was born.

In their organizing strategy, the BJNY steering committee tried to mirror the tactics employed in Oklahoma. They assembled local organizing committees in communities throughout the state, relying heavily on local League chapters to bring other organizations on board. They held kickoffs and tried to recruit public officials for the circles. They wrote a comprehensive fact book on the justice system. Organizers spent much of late 1999 and early 2000 crisscrossing the state to visit local organizations. In the first few months of 2000, about 2,500 people took part in almost 200 study circles in seventy-one communities throughout the state. The New York City circles, however, were a disappointment, attracting less than 100 participants. Unlike organizers in the other two states, the New York organizers had a very difficult time recruiting legislators. Only a few attended the local action forums, and none took part in the circles themselves.

Reform of the state's drug laws was one of the participants' principal concerns. Since 1973, when the New York legislature passed the so-called Rockefeller Drug Laws, creating some of the strictest mandatory minimum sentences for drug offenses in the country, the state's prison population has increased from 12,000 to 70,000 inmates. In 2000, the state spent $2.3 billion on its prison system. Of the offenders jailed for drug offenses, approximately 95 percent are people of color. Ninety-eight percent of the study circle reports called for the review, reform, or repeal of the Rockefeller Drug Laws. The BJNY participants also supported a renewed emphasis on rehabilitation in the corrections system, endorsed the expansion of parole, and championed an increase in funding and resources for crime prevention.

**Politics Is a Four-Letter Word.** At twenty-one action forums held throughout the state in April and May of 2000, fifty-five task forces were formed to work on issues such as crime prevention, drug law reform, public education on justice issues, restorative justice projects, the role of race in the criminal justice system, alternatives to incarceration, and support for prison families. On June 3, 2000, over 200 participants gathered in Albany for a statewide action forum; at that event, sixteen more task forces were formed, bringing people from different communities together to work on state-level issues.

As these task forces moved forward at the state and local levels in the summer of 2000, the participants displayed a savvy political sensibility. They didn't quit their jobs to lobby full-time, but they didn't shy away from politics either. The BJNY participants acted as though they had a natural role in the political process. They moved forward in ways that reaffirmed and expanded their aura of legitimacy, gave them a legitimate place in policymaking, and extended legitimacy to other citizens. This new spirit was evident in a number of ways.

*Citizens became regular members of the policymaking process in a particular issue area.* Many of the local and state task forces began holding meetings with public officials to work with them on policy issues. The state Task Force on Correctional Education linked up with an official in the state Department of Education, who in turn helped them set up a meeting between the task force and the representatives of several agencies that run education programs inside the prison system. The initial meeting was successful, and the group evolved into an entirely new and permanent task force made up of citizens and stakeholders in the justice system from all across the state. This group now has five subcommittees, dealing with transitional education services, libraries and new education technologies, postsecondary education, research and information sharing, and education of legislators and the public. Each subcommittee includes both citizens and stakeholders, but it was decided that only the citizens would cast votes on group decisions so that the officials wouldn't be accused of "politics." The BJNY participants clearly felt comfortable exercising their political legitimacy in this new role.

On a smaller scale, local task forces dealing with mental health issues began working with mental health officials and corrections officers in Albany and Rochester to establish new policies and programs for inmates with mental illnesses. In Albany the task force established relationships with the city's criminal court, the New York Mental Health Association, the Albany Police Department, and the Council of Community Services. The meetings have focused on developing a new model, based on a successful program in Wisconsin, for serving mentally ill people coming out of the corrections system or at risk of becoming involved with the system. The Rochester task force has enlisted the aid of the city's forensic court psychiatrist, the assistant probation administrator, and the state chapter of the National Association for the Mentally Ill. "We are forming alliances with significant individuals who make decisions that affect the care of the mentally ill . . . in the criminal justice system," said Donna Adams, chair of the Rochester effort.

In Schenectady, BJNY participants didn't have to forge new partnerships after the circles had ended; because several local judges and sheriffs participated in the program, the collaboration began in the circles themselves. The three task forces formed at the Schenectady County action forum already had public officials on board, and less than a year later a drug court and a youth court had been established. County sheriff Harry Buffardi said that those ideas were born in the circles, and developed quite quickly after the sessions concluded and the task forces began meeting. "From that it was like a snowball going downhill, picking up momentum and speed and people along the way," he said.

The way that BJNY participants approached these collaborations was telling and unusual. The task forces didn't stage protests or wage advocacy campaigns to sway policymakers—even though some of the participants were veteran activists used to more confrontational tactics. But neither did they just give polite input or offer to spend volunteer time on priorities already identified by the public officials. Instead, they formed relationships with officials and organized meetings that brought citizens and decision makers together. At those meetings the attendees all approached the issue from the same vantage point: as community members eager to solve a public problem.

*Citizens created new organizations and titles to strengthen and sustain their legitimacy.* As a whole, BJNY created more task forces—fifty-five at the local level, and sixteen at the state level—than any other democratic organizing effort has to date. By giving titles to these groups of people and by publicizing their work, the BJNY organizers took advantage of the power of legitimacy to strengthen and sustain citizen resolve.

In Albany one of the first concerns of the task force members was how to sustain their effort beyond one or two action projects. The Task Force on Community Involvement came up with a particularly creative solution: a new nonprofit and a new building to house it. First, they established a new non-profit organization, the Community Restoration, Arts, and Involvement Group (CRAIG), to help neighborhoods empower their residents, develop resources that preserve, promote, and protect their quality of life, and promote equality and respect for all. CRAIG's first signature project—and the one which it hopes will give the group a long-term home in community politics—is the restoration of a church to become the Old St. Anthony's Cultural Community Center. The building will include an ethnic heritage gallery, a performance stage, and offices for CRAIG. BJNY participants researched a similar project in Orlando, Florida, attained the support of the Policy Research Action Group at Loyola University in Chicago, and applied for urban rejuvenation funds from the city and state. Local craftspersons and workers will restore and maintain the property.

*Citizens helped to legitimize ideas that had not been given credibility before.* In at least two communities, BJNY participants were able to amplify ideas and voices that were being ignored by policymakers. When the circles got underway in Tompkins County, where Ithaca is located, the county board was considering a proposal to expand the county jail. A group called UNCAJE (United Citizens for Alternatives to Jail Expansion) had formed to oppose the plan; many citizens found out about UNCAJE through the circles, and a number decided to join the effort. In the first half of 2000, the effort to stop the jail expansion and provide resources for alternative sentencing gained critical mass. In June, the board decided against the expansion. The board also created an entirely new county department, the Department of Community Justice Services, and allocated almost $500,000 for a greatly expanded alternatives program that will include an evaluation component to verify its impact on crime and incarceration rates. The centerpiece of the plan, a new Community Justice Center, now provides assessment services, educational and computer training, job skills training, life skills training, and victim-offender mediation services. The program places "a strong emphasis on long-term crime prevention, with attention to programs for at-risk children," says Eric Lerner, chair of the UNCAJE steering committee. "Balancing Justice helped make it clear to elected officials that there is broad-based support for alternatives, and that they could not simply take for granted that voters wanted only clichés about 'getting tough' on crime," Lerner says.

The people who took part in Balancing Justice in New York were motivated by an interest in public issues. At least some came in with a determination to change how their communities and their state dealt with offenders. Perhaps the greatest change wrought by the program, however, was in the relationship between these citizens and the political process. BJNY gave them a greater sense of membership in the political system, and in the months after their participation in the dialogues, their participation in action efforts reflected their changed status. Some sought to affirm and extend their new-found legitimacy, others used it to affect policy decisions, and still others tried to bring previously excluded voices into political debates.

## Creating Opportunities to Sustain Participation

The democratic organizers in Oklahoma, Minnesota, and New York reaffirmed the political importance of active citizenship. They sent a clear and inspiring message about what citizens could achieve, what was expected of them, and what they could expect from the political process. This message was a call to arms, a job announcement, and a promissory note all rolled into one. These programs made it clear that citizens can do more than just vote: they can take part in dialogue and deliberation, help make decisions, and take action themselves.

Realizing this more active concept of citizenship on a broader scale will require more than just a well-crafted national recruitment pitch. Bush administration officials talk of establishing a "civic switchboard" of volunteerism opportunities, but you can't recruit people by waiting for them to call. The recent explosion of study circle programs has been driven by democratic organizers working in communities, reaching into the groups and organizations people belong to, and engaging them with the promise of action on issues they care about. Although democratic organizers can create settings where citizens and public officials can work together through dialogue and action, these opportunities for participatory governance are only temporary. They are fragile, ad hoc efforts rather than stable, enduring institutions. Once the circles conclude, once the task forces finish their work, citizens find themselves without a home in the policymaking process. The Bush administration and its new civic corps could build on the principles of democratic organizing by helping communities create durable new structures for citizen involvement.

The fate of HB 1213 in the Oklahoma legislature illustrates the need for some institutionalized means for continued citizen participation. After the bill passed, the legislature bogged down in arguments over when it would take effect and whether it should be fully funded. The same lobbyists who had helped create the legislative train wrecks before 1996 went to work again, turning the screws on legislators. On the campaign trail, new candidates used the same old rhetoric about crime to scare the voters. Finally, in a special session in 1999, the legislature gutted much of the bill, removing most offenses from the truth-in-sentencing requirements and appropriating a much smaller amount for community corrections projects. According to the members of the Oklahoma League of Women Voters who have followed the process, the Oklahoma corrections system is better off than it was in the early 1990s, but it is not as improved as it would have been if HB 1213 had survived intact.

At the local level, many of the people who came together for Balancing Justice in Oklahoma are still working together, and community corrections projects continue to grow. But at the state level, once the circles stopped meeting, the unprecedented unity of citizens, professionals, and public officials began to fall apart. The sense of political legitimacy for average citizens began to dissipate too.

"My main regret is that we lost track of the process," says Judge Jacqueline Duncan. "We didn't realize that the way we got people involved was as important as what they said in those discussions. We should've recognized the true value of Balancing Justice—that citizens and government were working together—and found ways of making that a regular, permanent part of the way we made decisions and solved problems."

In study circles and other democratic organizing projects, citizens across the country have demonstrated the will to take an active role in problem solving. To sustain this energy and commitment we need to change our political system to make it more hospitable to citizen involvement. Democratic organizers should establish regular opportunities for individuals to make public statements, take part in dialogue, find common ground with people of opposing views, make bargains, demonstrate their loyalty and love of community, give meaningful input on decisions, and contribute their own effort, ideas, and time to solving problems. This collective capacity for deliberation and decision making is an essential resource for addressing public problems that we must not let rest underutilized.

*Matt Leighninger is a senior associate with the Study Circles Resource Center.*

# Public Participation in Environmental Decision Making: Is It Working?

*Matthew McKinney, Will Harmon*

> The point of public participation is that by adding the value-rich perspectives of citizens to the information-rich perspectives of experts, we can create wiser public policy.
>
> —Adapted from Daniel Yankelovich, *The Magic of Dialogue*

Since the National Environmental Policy Act (NEPA) was passed in 1969, public participation has been an important component of environmental planning and decision making.[1] Under NEPA and state environmental policy acts,[2] public officials are required to notify the public and offer them an opportunity to comment on proposed environmental decisions. During the past thirty years, scholars and practitioners have developed a variety of processes to inform and educate the public and to seek their input and advice.[3] Although many of these processes provide innovative means for public participation, the ongoing challenge for public officials is to integrate the often conflicting values and interests of citizens with the complex scientific and technical aspects of environmental decisions.

Perhaps symptomatic of that challenge, public participation under NEPA and similar state acts has been criticized from every angle. While many proposals are publicly scrutinized and processed with relatively little fanfare, project proponents sometimes complain of unwarranted and costly delays. The public argues that it is not given ample time to reflect and comment or that comments are collected but not heeded. For their part, responsible agencies say that they are overworked and understaffed, and that dwindling budgets are further tapped by public participation requirements. These criticisms raise an obvious question about whether public participation is working in these circumstances, yet there has been surprisingly little critical analysis of the effectiveness of public participation under NEPA and state environmental policy acts.[4]

In 1999, after debating several proposals to change the Montana Environmental Policy Act (MEPA),[5] the Montana Legislature concluded that the magnitude and complexity of the issues related to MEPA and its implementation required a careful, reflective, deliberative study. As a result, the legislature adopted Senate Joint Resolution No. 18 requesting the legislative Environmental Quality Council (EQC) to "conduct an interim study of the Montana Environmental Policy Act."[6] As part of the study, section 1(c) of the joint resolution asked EQC to examine the degree to which MEPA "results in government accountability" and "Montanans are informed of and participate in state agency decisions." Section 3(c) directs EQC to consider "whether citizens are effectively participating in the MEPA decision making processes."

To help achieve these tasks, EQC asked the Montana Consensus Council (MCC) to evaluate the effectiveness of public participation under MEPA. MCC, an independent nonprofit organization administratively attached to the Office of the Governor, agreed and started by reviewing the literature and developing a framework to evaluate the effectiveness of public participation. The purpose of this article is to report on whether public participation in environmental decision making is working, at least as it is applied in Montana, and how it can be improved.

## Methodology

Based on a review of the literature, consultations with scholars interested in evaluating public participation and public dispute resolution processes, and the specific concerns articulated in Senate Joint Resolution No. 18, MCC developed a survey questionnaire that allows citizens, project proponents, and public officials to evaluate the effectiveness of public participation from their own perspectives. In addition to a few methodological questions, we asked participants to

1. Identify the most important objectives of public involvement.
2. Evaluate the degree to which public involvement is timely, cost effective, and efficient.
3. Assess whether all identifiable stakeholders have the opportunity and are encouraged to take part in public involvement processes.
4. Reflect on whether citizens and stakeholders do participate in public involvement processes.
5. Consider whether stakeholders, including project proponents and the responsible agency, have an opportunity through public involvement processes to learn about each other's interests and concerns.
6. Examine the degree to which the responsible agency fairly and accurately incorporates public comments into decisions.
7. Evaluate the degree to which public input and advice improves the quality of the proposed project and results in better decisions.
8. Identify and explain ways to improve public participation under MEPA.

A draft of the survey questionnaire was circulated to professional colleagues, EQC staff, and EQC members for their input and advice. In January 2000, MCC mailed the survey to about 280 people, including citizens, project proponents, Montana state agencies, local government offices, federal agencies, conservation groups, law firms, and the university system. The mailing list was compiled by EQC and included people and organizations that participated in or commented on past MEPA-related actions.

By the end of January 2000, MCC had received only 55 responses, so we mailed cards to people who had not yet responded, asking them to complete the survey and return it. As of February 23, 2000, we had received 96 surveys, 3 of which were left blank. The numbers that follow in this article do not always add up to 93 because not everyone responded to every part of the survey. Percentages may not add up to 100 because of rounding.

## Who Responded?

In analyzing responses to the survey, we took people at their word when they wrote on the survey that they were representing themselves as private citizens, rather than responding on behalf of some organization or other affiliation. Readers should also recognize that individual responses from agencies and other organizations may not represent an official position.

Of the 93 completed surveys, 17 percent were filled out by state agency staff and administrators—the people responsible for conducting public involvement projects under MEPA. The remaining 83 percent were filled out by the people MEPA-driven public involvement is meant to serve, the project proponents, including citizens, conservation groups, and representatives of business and industry. Table 1 presents a detailed list of respondents, which can be categorized into the following stakeholder groups:

| | |
|---|---|
| Conservation organizations | 22 (24%) |
| Independent citizens | 21 (23%) |
| Representatives of business and industry | 17 (18%) |
| Local and federal agencies, the university system, church-affiliated groups, and law firms | 17 (18%) |
| State agencies | 16 (17%) |

Although this study likely captures the input and advice of people and organizations that account for a significant majority of those who participate in MEPA-driven public involvement processes, other perspectives may not be represented here. Survey respondents are not a random sample of Montanans; the findings of this research represent the thoughts and views of a relatively narrow, vested set of interests—people who have participated in or commented on past MEPA-related actions. Of the 93 people who filled out all or most of the survey, 37 said they had participated in one to five MEPA-driven public

## Table 1.  Survey Respondents

*Conservation Groups*

Bear Creek Council
Big Hole Watershed Committee
Citizens for a Better Flathead
Fishing Outfitters Association of Montana
Friends of the Rocky Mountain Front
Friends of the Wild Swan
Gallatin Valley Land Trust
Greater Yellowstone Coalition
Keep Montana Clean and Beautiful
Medicine River Canoe Club
Montana Audubon Society
Montana Ecosystem Defense Council
Montana Environmental Information Center
Montana River Action Network
Montana Trout Unlimited
Montana Wilderness Association
Montana Wildlife Federation
Public Lands Access Association

*Citizens Representing Themselves, by Locality (Number of Individuals)*

| | |
|---|---|
| Unidentified | (2) |
| Billings | (1) |
| Bozeman | (2) |
| Great Falls | (6) |
| Helena | (1) |
| Indiana | (1) |
| Kalispell | (1) |
| Miles City | (1) |
| Missoula | (3) |
| St. Regis | (1) |
| Stockett | (1) |

*Businesses and Industry Associations*

ASARCO Incorporated
EHS Services, Inc.
Express Pipeline
Exxon Mobile Billings Refinery
IMP
Land and Water Consulting, Inc.
Montana Alternative Livestock Producers
Montana Building Industry Association
Montana Farm Bureau
Montana Logging Association
Montana Power Company
Montana Refining Company
Montana Resources
Montana Stockgrowers Association

*(continued)*

## Table 1. (continued)

*Businesses and Industry Associations*

Montana Wood Products Association
WBI Holdings, Inc.
Western Environmental Trade Association
WGM Group

*Federal Agencies*

U.S. Bureau of Land Management
U.S. Department of Agriculture, Natural Resources
Conservation Service
U.S. Environmental Protection Agency

*Local Government*

Butte-Silver Bow Local Government Extension Service
Gallatin County Commissioner
Jefferson County
Missoula Health Department
Ravalli County Planning Board

*Other*

Browning Law Firm
Gough, Shanahan, Johnson, and Waterman
Montana Association of Churches
Montana Catholic Conference
University of Montana School of Law

*State Agencies*

Montana Department of Agriculture
Montana Department of Environmental Quality
Montana Department of Fish, Wildlife and Parks
Montana Department of Military Affairs
Montana Department of Natural Resources and Conservation
Montana Department of Transportation
Montana Natural Resource Information System

involvement processes, 17 said six to ten processes, and 35 said ten or more processes. Three people reported that they had not participated in any such process. Their survey responses were presumably based on personal interest as outside observers or as potential participants in the future.

Sixty-five survey respondents (72 percent) said they were basing their responses on a synthesis of many experiences with MEPA processes. Several people said that their frame of reference included processes that combined MEPA and NEPA. Some people also based their responses on experiences with how MEPA-driven public involvement is typically conducted, whereas others based their responses, at least in part, on an idealized vision of how they think public involvement *should* be conducted under MEPA.

## Major Themes

Eight themes emerge from an analysis of the survey responses. These themes are presented here as a synthesis of what people said in responding to the survey.

THEME 1. *The idea of public involvement under MEPA is good public policy, but the practice of public involvement under MEPA could be improved.*

Of the 93 people who completed surveys, 88 percent responded favorably toward the idea of public involvement in MEPA-driven decisions. Public involvement is good policy, they said, because it: brings additional and often valuable information to light that might not be heard otherwise; can help produce better proposals and decisions; provides important opportunities to exchange information among stakeholders, project proponents, and responsible agencies; creates opportunities for public disclosure of proposed projects, potential impacts, and alternatives; and may identify problems and build understanding about projects and potential impacts while there is still time to consider alternatives, including mitigation.

Many people, however, also said that the practice of public involvement under MEPA does not always live up to its promise. A common comment was, "MEPA is fine, but agencies need to improve the way public involvement under MEPA is implemented." Survey respondents cited a number of areas they say need improvement, including better public notification of upcoming projects; a more consistent and structured approach to public involvement from one agency to the next; broader recognition by agencies that social, cultural, aesthetic, and natural values are as substantive as economic and scientific data; and a better effort by agencies to clearly show how public comment is incorporated into decision making.

Some survey respondents (11 people, or approximately 11 percent) were less enchanted with the idea of public involvement in MEPA-driven decisions. They wrote that public involvement is costly and time consuming, and it adds little value because comments tend toward rhetoric and emotion rather than science and substance. They said that the key issues and concerns are often known in advance, and little or no new information is gained from public involvement. Several people said that public comment tends to be one-sided— against proposed projects—and that people with an ax to grind can delay or block projects, or make them unprofitable, at no cost to themselves.

THEME 2. *Members of the general public are uninterested in most MEPA projects, or do not believe that their input will make a difference. Some people do not understand the purpose of MEPA and how it works. Consequently, few independent citizens participate in MEPA processes, which tend to be dominated by project proponents and organized interest groups.*

Most survey respondents (72 percent) said that people do participate in MEPA-driven public involvement, and that participation varies widely (and sometimes unpredictably) from project to project. Several survey respondents said that while the numbers of people submitting comments may vary, nevertheless it is usually the same people and groups that participate. Widespread public participation is uncommon. One person said that conservation groups are effective "watchdogs" for the general public.

In general, more people participate when a proposed project requires an environmental impact statement (EIS), when significant environmental resources or values may be affected, when the proposed project would be located near a population center, and when interest groups stir up a controversy. Several people said that some agencies conduct "checklist" environmental assessments (EAs), which tend to minimize opportunities for public involvement. They also said that public participation is discouraged when notices of proposed projects and their locations are described only in technical or legal terms.

Several people said that to encourage more widespread participation, the general public needs more and better information about MEPA's purpose, about how public involvement is conducted, and about proposed projects and the responsible agency's decision-making process.[7]

THEME 3. *The objectives of public involvement under MEPA need to be clarified. This will help agencies, project proponents, stakeholders, and the general public develop a common understanding of the purpose of MEPA and MEPA-driven public involvement.*

Survey responses revealed an apparent split in perceptions of the purpose and intent of MEPA. Some people said that the purpose was for the agency to adequately examine and disclose to the public the environmental impacts of a proposed action and its alternatives. This may create opportunities for agencies and proponents to gain an understanding of the different goals each may have in permitting a project, but such opportunities are secondary, a byproduct of the process rather than its primary aim. This view of the process emphasizes the agency's role as an information source and decision maker.

Other people said MEPA's purpose is to discover the interests and concerns of stakeholders and the general public regarding a proposed project. They said this gives decision makers the benefit of interdisciplinary and public review of a proposal so that all the pros and cons are fleshed out. This view of the process emphasizes the public's role as an information source and adviser to decisions that affect public resources and the human environment.

Even among state agencies this split is apparent. Some agency staff use the opportunities created by MEPA to engage in a dialogue with the public and stakeholders. Others said that public comments do help inform agencies, but an actual face-to-face conversation is better. Public meetings, they said, are conducive to such exchanges. Other state agency personnel are less inclined toward hosting such dialogue. They see their role as recipients of comments from project proponents and opponents, not as a bridge between the two.

This split has generated apparent frustration over the lack of a clear, generally accepted purpose for public involvement under MEPA. When asked to rank the importance of six different objectives for public involvement under MEPA, people varied widely in their responses. Five of the six objectives received ten or more votes for ranking highest in importance (Table 2). And although a clear majority (62 percent) of people ranked "resolve conflict among competing interests" as least important, three people ranked this objective highest. Several people commented that ranking these objectives was difficult because all of them are important.

The fact that the rankings are scattered relatively evenly among five of the six objectives suggests either that people expect public involvement under MEPA to serve more than one purpose, or that at least in some people's minds, the objectives of public involvement are not clear. Is public involvement under MEPA intended simply as an opportunity for agencies to provide information and education? Or is the intent to seek public input and advice? At the far end of the public involvement continuum, should we expect the process to resolve conflicts among competing interests?

## Table 2. Ranking the Importance of Objectives of Public Involvement Under MEPA

| Objectives | 1 (highest) | 2 | 3 | 4 | 5 | 6 (lowest) |
|---|---|---|---|---|---|---|
| Provide information and education | 19 | 18 | 23 | 11 | 10 | 5 |
| Seek public input and advice | 27 | 21 | 18 | 11 | 7 | 1 |
| Promote mutual understanding of the substantive issues | 10 | 16 | 13 | 26 | 15 | 2 |
| Increase the quality of the project and final decisions | 32 | 20 | 7 | 12 | 7 | 6 |
| Foster trust, communication, and understanding among stakeholders, including agencies | 14 | 7 | 10 | 12 | 22 | 18 |
| Resolve conflict among competing interests | 3 | 3 | 5 | 12 | 14 | 53 |

Note: The numbers in this table indicate the number of times each objective was ranked 1, 2, 3, and so on. For example, "seek public input and advice" was ranked first 27 times, second 21 times, third 18 times, and so forth.

Overall, survey respondents clearly ranked three objectives highest in importance (see Table 2):

1. Increase the quality of the project and final decisions.
2. Seek public input and advice.
3. Provide information and education.

It's worth noting that if we look at the four main categories of respondents, the split described above becomes more apparent. For citizens representing themselves, the three most important objectives were the same as for the overall group, and conservation groups simply flipped the first and second objectives. State agencies and representatives of business and industry (project proponents), however, said the most important objective was to provide information and education. Both of the latter groups also gave a high ranking to promoting mutual understanding of substantive issues.

Most people gave a strong last place ranking to "resolve conflict among competing interests." Apparently, most people do not expect MEPA to be a conflict resolution process, nor are most agencies eager to accept such a task.

THEME 4. *The quality of public involvement processes varies widely from case to case and from agency to agency. There should be a consistent, structured approach across all state agencies.*

Many people said that there are as many formats for public involvement as there are state agencies conducting them. This often leads to confusion and misunderstandings among stakeholders, including project proponents. In the survey, we asked state agencies whether they possessed written policies and procedures for public involvement under MEPA. The Departments of Fish, Wildlife and Parks (DFWP); Natural Resources and Conservation (DNRC); and Agriculture all said they refer to the Administrative Rules of Montana. DFWP also provided copies of several interoffice memorandums on MEPA compliance and an EA checklist. The Department of Transportation (MDT) said it has a public involvement handbook. The Department of Environmental Quality (DEQ) reported that staff are currently drafting written policy. The Department of Military Affairs said it follows guidelines in Army Regulation 200-2 on the environmental effects of Army actions.

Survey respondents offered several ideas on how to make public involvement more consistent and uniform from one agency to the next: make public notification requirements uniform; require public meetings in all MEPA processes; set a standard EA and EIS comment period for all agencies (most suggested a thirty-day comment period for all EAs and a sixty-day period for all EISs, while one person said a minimum ninety-day period should be required for all MEPA projects); and make it easier for project sponsors to work with one or two responsible agencies, rather than many.

Many people also said that the public involvement process should be easier to understand and take part in, and that it should be more structured. They suggested a variety of strategies for doing this, some of which would streamline the structure while others would add new components, such as facilitation and additional documentation. Suggested strategies included these: (1) Because unstructured processes can go awry, make sure public involvement is *facilitated* by an impartial third party. (2) Small groups, such as focus groups, advisory committees, and field tours, should be used to encourage a detailed, informed discussion of the issues and alternatives at hand. This saves time and money, and improves the quality of the decision making. (3) Agencies should provide better summaries—balanced and science based, with references cited—on the issues and decisions at hand. (4) Agencies should summarize all public comments and distribute copies to all participants, so people know they have been heard. (5) Agencies should agree on standard definitions of "significant" and "cumulative impacts." (6) Unnecessary delays should be avoided by fixing a finite time for comments and responses. Hold people and organizations responsible for delays by making them liable for any costs incurred. (7) Require agencies to respond only to substantive comments. (8) Publish success stories of how public involvement has improved projects and decision making.

THEME 5. *Montanans have opportunities to participate in state agency decisions, but public notification about upcoming MEPA projects needs to be improved, and state agencies should do more to encourage public participation.*

Most survey respondents (69 percent) generally agree that stakeholders have opportunities and are encouraged to participate in public involvement processes under MEPA. Legal notices are published in newspapers, they said, and state agencies take public comments in writing and also directly at meetings. Several people pointed out that participation requires some initiative from the stakeholders to find out about a project proposal and the request for comments. One respondent from business and industry said that environmental groups effectively track MEPA projects and act as citizen watchdogs when members of the general public do not participate.

Even among the people who felt that opportunities for participation were adequate, however, many said that agencies need to do more than run small legal notices in local newspapers. Such notices, they said, typically fill an inch or two of column space, are buried within the newspaper, and are easy to miss. Suggestions for improving public notice included working with reporters to generate feature stories, posting notices on a central MEPA web site, doing public service announcements on radio and television, and setting up a telephone hot line with project announcements and information on how to submit comments. Some complained that the legal descriptions of property given in most notices are difficult to understand, and the public would be better served by "real-world" descriptions written in plain language.

Twenty-three survey respondents (26 percent) said that opportunities and encouragement for public involvement were not adequate. Many of these people said that public notification and encouragement varies widely from one state agency to the next, and that this lack of consistency or uniformity is a problem in itself. "Unless a group is signed up to receive MEPA notices, it's almost impossible to find out what is going on," one respondent reported.

Several people said that in some cases agencies have done a good job of contacting stakeholders and providing ample opportunities for comment, but sometimes agencies act as though they want to discourage public involvement. One person alleged that the Montana Department of Transportation "skips MEPA notice requirements by getting a categorical exclusion from MEPA and then following NEPA, which has its own notice requirements. It is therefore frustrating and impossible to follow MEPA compliance at MDT." A number of independent citizens and people representing conservation groups complained about what they characterized as the ongoing inadequacy of public involvement processes conducted by the Oil and Gas Conservation Division at DNRC. Oil and Gas proposals, said one respondent, have been "particularly clandestine."

Several people said that agencies may provide opportunities for public involvement, but seldom do they actually *encourage* participation. Several others wrote that many incentives (workload, budget and staff constraints, and political pressure) drive agencies to streamline the MEPA process, so it's better for them to minimize public involvement. A few people also said that "stakeholders" is too narrow a term—that MEPA is about *public* participation. Too often, they said, agencies want to involve only those with an economic interest in the proposed project. They worried that when agencies are responsible for identifying stakeholders, they may "stack the deck," resulting in a surfeit of one-sided comments.

State agencies, on the other hand, said that they do a good job of providing opportunities and encouragement for stakeholder participation in public involvement processes under MEPA. Some agency personnel wrote that they "go beyond what is necessary" to involve the public. Several state agency respondents said that a news release was adequate notice. In contrast, one official with DNRC said that a properly conducted public involvement process should include public scoping, informational meetings, and hearings. Another person at DNRC replied that citizen interests are not often incorporated, and organized special interest groups dominate the public involvement process— a concern voiced by other state agencies and other survey respondents. Finally, two agency responses (both from DNRC) indicated some frustration that the process may be too open to public participation, one questioning how the term *stakeholders* should be defined: "Anyone with an interest—or someone that is truly impacted by a proposed action?"

THEME 6. *The quality of public comment needs to be improved. Comments should be substantive and based on the best available information. But agencies need to provide better, more timely information to educate citizens. They must also show serious consideration for comments and recognize that less tangible environmental values (such as social, cultural, aesthetic, and natural values) are just as substantive as economic values and scientific information.*

One independent citizen and several people within state agencies and business and industry said that the bulk of public comments are often not substantive or relevant, and suggested that when projects are highly technical, few members of the general public are knowledgeable enough to understand them. But most citizens and people representing conservation groups said that project proponents and responsible agencies do not always provide good, timely information on which to base comments. Often, they said, the information is unnecessarily technical, legal, or otherwise hard to understand. People complained that, in some cases, project proponents and agencies do not fully disclose the nature of the project or its potential impacts. Public comment, said one person, is only as good as the information provided by the project proponents and agencies.

People also said that most agencies show a bias toward scientific and economic data, too often dismissing substantive comments based on social, cultural, aesthetic, and natural values. Public comment, they said, does not have to come from experts or economically vested interests to produce valuable improvements to the proposed project. People wrote that agencies and project proponents should make a good faith effort to fully disclose all relevant information to the public, and do so before the formal public involvement process begins. Several people also said that public comment would improve if more time was allowed to review and comment on draft EAs and EISs.

THEME 7. *Although state agencies seek public input and advice, they don't always listen to what is said. The process of incorporating public comment into MEPA analysis, making trade-offs among competing interests, and integrating public input and scientific information should be more transparent, participatory, and interactive.*

Survey respondents were divided down the middle when asked whether responsible agencies fairly and accurately incorporate public comments into decisions. Forty-four percent said that, in general, agencies do fairly and accurately incorporate comments, while 42 percent disagreed (14 percent were indifferent). Interestingly, state, local, and federal agencies said that comments are fairly and accurately incorporated, while most conservation groups, business and industry, and citizens disagreed.

Written comments in response to this question indicated a range of expectations for incorporating public comment under MEPA. Some people said that MEPA does not require "fair and accurate" incorporation of comments into the decision. Under MEPA, they argued, an agency must provide the rationale for its decision, which should in effect document the "fairness" of the decision.

Others felt that agencies must show that public comment was seriously considered. They voiced frustration over instances in which they say agency decisions disregarded substantive information from public comment. Between these two extremes, many people said that stakeholders, the agencies, and project proponents all bear responsibility for improving the relevance and content of public comment.

For substantive comments to be acknowledged and incorporated into the analysis and decision, agencies, project proponents, and other stakeholders must be willing to engage in a genuine exchange of information, a process of mutual learning. Apparently, opportunities for such an exchange do exist. Most people (77 percent) agreed with the statement that "The stakeholders, including project proponents and the responsible agency, have an opportunity through public involvement processes under MEPA to learn about each other's interests and concerns."

Nevertheless, many people cited difficulties, chief among them a tendency toward rhetoric and posturing that overshadows genuine discussion and disclosure of real issues. People also said that agencies and stakeholder groups may be locked into their positions and are unwilling to seriously consider what others have to offer. Representatives of conservation groups said that mutual learning would be made easier if public involvement occurred earlier in the process, allowing comment on the purpose and need of the proposed action. This might also prevent the "us versus them" mentality that sometimes arises when agencies and project proponents begin working together long before the public is involved. Finally, comments from state agencies indicated that fostering dialogue is low on the long list of agency priorities. Existing staffing levels make it difficult to implement all aspects of MEPA because of the time required to prepare MEPA documents.

THEME 8. *Public involvement is a critical ingredient of MEPA. The associated costs and perceived delays in the decision-making process are outweighed by the benefits of informing the public, gathering input, and securing public understanding of and support for projects.*

The survey asked people whether they agreed or disagreed that public involvement under MEPA is timely, cost effective, and efficient. About 56 percent of respondents agreed that the public involvement process is timely. About 48 percent agreed that it is cost effective, while only about 40 percent agreed that it is efficient. The "indifferent" check-off drew more responses for this statement than for any other statement in the survey (16 percent for timely, 32 percent for cost effective, and 25 percent for efficient). This may reflect a low interest or level of concern with these qualities—several people noted that public involvement was so essential that it should not be measured by its cost effectiveness or efficiency. Others felt that only the agencies know how much such processes cost and how much time is involved, so they are unqualified to answer. Some people said these qualities depend to a high degree on which agency is involved, and others said it depends on the nature of the project.

The survey also asked people to rank ten issues related to public participation under MEPA in order of their importance. The two lowest rankings were given to "delays associated with public involvement," and "the costs associated with public involvement." Several people said that delays and costs associated with public involvement are outweighed by the benefits of informing the public, gathering input, and securing public understanding of and support for projects.

Most survey respondents (74 percent) agreed that public input improves the proposed project and results in better decisions. Some indicated that this was "obvious" or "always" the case. Others said that the degree of improvement varies from project to project, depending in part on the complexity of the project. A few people said that public input does *not* result in better projects and decisions, but only because the agencies disregard the input. They said that public comments often provide valuable information and a broader perspective on how to improve projects, and agencies need to include such input in their decisions.

## Recommendations

Based on the survey findings and a review of best practices for public participation, MCC suggested a number of recommendations to EQC to improve public participation under MEPA. EQC members and staff reviewed and discussed these recommendations at length during meetings that were open to the public. They heard public comment on MCC's recommendations and asked for clarifications from MCC staff as they deliberated whether to adopt each recommendation.

In its final report to the legislature, EQC found that "the idea of public involvement under MEPA is good public policy. Public involvement is a critical ingredient of MEPA. The practice of public involvement under MEPA needs to be improved."[8] EQC then adopted nearly every recommendation of MCC. One blanket change made by EQC was to encourage agencies to amend their administrative rules for MEPA compliance to incorporate the recommendations, rather than amending the MEPA statute or model rules, as suggested by MCC. A closer look at each recommendation and EQC's rationale for its modifications offers a glimpse of how a group of lawmakers and citizens relied on public input to suggest improvements to public participation under MEPA.

MCC RECOMMENDATION 1. *Amend the MEPA statute to clarify the value of public involvement under MEPA (see themes 3 and 8).*

In making this recommendation, MCC noted that public participation in state government decision making is mandated under Article II, Section 8 of

Montana's constitution and in statutes (Montana Code Annotated [MCA] 2-3-101). MEPA requires that agencies make information on proposed actions available to the public, with the intent of promoting informed decision making.

The results of the survey indicate that most people believe public involvement is a critical ingredient for the successful implementation of MEPA. Public participation, however, is not mentioned in the "Purpose" section of MEPA (MCA 75-1-102). Further, survey results indicate that the value and purpose of MEPA-driven public involvement need to be clarified. Therefore, MCC suggested that the legislature should amend the law to include a statement of the value of public involvement under MEPA.

EQC members were reluctant, however, to tinker with the statute, suggesting that doing so might open MEPA to other, less moderate amendments from all sides. Instead, they recommended revising the MEPA-relevant administrative rules of state agencies to include statements clarifying the purpose and value of public participation (which are provided in MCC's second recommendation).

MCC RECOMMENDATION 2. *Clarify the value and purpose of public involvement under MEPA.*

Given the lack of consensus on the value and purpose of public involvement under MEPA, MCC suggested that EQC amend the statute and model MEPA rules to include the following statement of values for public participation:

- The public should have a say in decisions about actions that affect people's lives.
- Public participation should be based on the premise that the public's contribution will influence the decision.
- The public participation process communicates the interests and meets the process needs of all participants.
- The public participation process seeks out and facilitates the involvement of people who are potentially affected.
- The public participation process involves participants in defining how they participate.
- The public participation process provides participants with the information they need to participate in a meaningful way.
- The public participation process communicates to participants how their input affected the decision.

These value statements are adapted from survey responses and from the International Association for Public Participation.[9] EQC adopted this recommendation unchanged.

MCC RECOMMENDATION 3. *Amend the MEPA model rules to provide a consistent approach to public involvement under MEPA across agencies and projects (see theme 4).*

MCC suggested four specific changes to the MEPA model rules. First, agencies should be encouraged to develop a public participation plan for every EA and EIS. MCC also offered guidance for public officials on how to articulate and agree on the objectives of public participation, and in turn to better match the process to achieve the objective.[10]

Second, agencies should be encouraged to use MCC, a state agency that specializes in public participation and conflict resolution, to help develop public participation plans. Third, state policy should require a public meeting or some other type of opportunity for citizens to interact with the agency and the project proponent on all EISs. Fourth, there should be a thirty-day public comment period on all EAs and a sixty-day public comment period on all EISs, unless the project proponent or a group of citizens requests a longer period in writing. If a request is made to extend the public comment period, the agency must justify in writing its decision to grant or deny the request.

EQC did not formally adopt the first three of these recommendations. One EQC member said that he was uncomfortable trying to "micro-manage" how agencies conduct public participation and that some agencies have already incorporated these ideas into their MEPA practices. EQC focused instead on lengthening the public comment period on draft EISs from thirty to sixty days and clarifying the rules for extending or shortening comment periods for EAs and EISs.

MCC RECOMMENDATION 4. *Amend the MEPA model rules to encourage "best practices" for public involvement under MEPA (see themes 1, 4, and 5).*

Scholars and practitioners have developed an impressive array of strategies, tools, and techniques to inform and educate citizens, seek input and advice, and to build agreement. To help public officials and decision makers improve the timing and meaningfulness of public participation, MCC provided a list of public participation strategies[11] and a checklist of collaborative strategies for public participation under MEPA (and NEPA). EQC members acknowledged the importance of such best practices by modifying this recommendation to require agencies to report back to EQC on the use of these best practices. EQC also wanted "more specific agency guidance on effective comments" in the agency administrative rules. They encouraged agencies to provide "better, more timely information (earlier in the process) to educate citizens," and to recognize that social, cultural, aesthetic, and natural values are "as worthy of consideration" as scientific and economic data.[12]

MCC RECOMMENDATION 5. *Amend the MEPA model rules to improve public awareness of MEPA and opportunities to participate (see themes 2 and 5).*

MCC suggested three specific strategies to achieve this goal: create a web site dedicated to MEPA, develop a single interagency brochure on public involvement opportunities under MEPA, and require agencies to distribute press releases or feature stories on every proposed project that requires an EIS. The thrust of these recommendations was to encourage agencies to move beyond reliance on small legal notices in newspapers and instead take advantage of other available media.

EQC members agreed and suggested that the EQC itself should create the central MEPA web site, with links to established agency MEPA web sites. They recommended that agencies without such web sites should create them and include updates on MEPA project implementation.

MCC RECOMMENDATION 6. *Amend the MEPA model rules to provide a more transparent, participatory, and interactive process to integrate public input and scientific information (see theme 7).*

In many respects, this recommendation cuts to the core of the practice of public participation under MEPA. Section XI, 2-3, of the MEPA model rules requires agencies to include in EISs "a list of all sources of written and oral comments on the draft EIS, including those obtained at public hearings, and, unless impractical, the text of comments received by the agency (in all cases, a representative sample of comments must be included)"; and "the agency's responses to substantive comments, including an evaluation of the comments received and disposition of the issues involved." The survey revealed, however, that citizens—including project proponents, interest groups, and independent citizens—are not satisfied with the degree to which their input and advice is reflected in agency decisions. As students of public participation know, this is not an unfamiliar criticism of public processes that are designed to only inform and educate the public, or to seek public input and advice.[13]

To improve this situation, MCC recommended that the legislature require some type of public involvement activity that allows the public to validate the agency's attempt to fairly and accurately incorporate public input and scientific information. For example, use a task force of citizens, project proponents, and agency officials to review and incorporate public comments; or use a feedback panel to review the agency's attempt to incorporate public comment. Such strategies are consistent with the collaborative learning model of public participation and dispute resolution.

EQC members were quick to support this recommendation, recognizing that it would serve the dual purpose of holding agencies accountable to the public while helping the public understand the rationale behind agency decisions. They recommended that agency administrative rules be amended to require some type of annual public involvement and feedback activity. The idea of a yearly public review of MEPA decisions was promoted as a means to look at agency decisions case by case, and also to reflect on an agency's track record and procedures across several projects at once.

## Public Participation in the Twenty-First Century

Based on this evaluation of Montana's experience, does public participation in environmental decision making work? The answer, of course, is mixed. Even after nearly 30 years of experience, the advice of Professor Arnold Bolle, former dean of the University of Montana's School of Forestry, seems relevant. In 1971, just after NEPA was signed into law, he said, "Effective public participation within the decision process is vital to environmental quality."[14] He went on to say that effective public participation will require innovative and adaptive processes, a greater understanding among all people of the issues and public decision making processes, and above all, patience. Along with patience, we would add perseverance.

The tools, techniques, and strategies for meaningful, effective public participation are available. The ideas of collaborative problem solving, consensus building,[15] and deliberative democracy[16] have come to the forefront of discussions about public dialogue and public decision making. The premise of these approaches is that, if the appropriate people—citizens and officials—come together in constructive forums with good information, they will create fair, effective, efficient public policy.[17]

These approaches are slowly being integrated into local, state, and federal systems of public decision making. Federal land agencies now promote "collaborative stewardship."[18] In fact, the recently adopted regulations guiding the revision of national forest management plans call for more collaborative approaches to public participation. In December 2000, the U.S. Environmental Protection Agency (EPA) released its draft Public Involvement Policy, which provides "guidance to EPA officials on effective means to involve the public in its regulatory and program decisions."[19] Federal and state agencies increasingly employ these ideas in negotiated rulemaking.[20] The Western Governors' Association has adopted two policies endorsing the use of consensus-building processes to shape public policy and resolve public disputes.[21] Three other regional political associations—the Council of State Governments-West (legislators), the Western Interstate Region of the National Association of Counties, and the Western Municipal Conference—have adopted a joint policy resolution on the role of collaborative problem solving in western natural resources.[22] And governors in several states have adopted executive orders promoting collaborative, consensus-based approaches to public participation and public dispute resolution.[23]

In addition to these policies, citizens themselves are creating new forums to exchange ideas, build understanding, and seek agreement on common problems. Throughout the country, particularly in the American West, many citizen-driven initiatives are emerging.[24] These efforts are variously referred to as community-based conservation, watershed councils, study groups, forestry partnerships, and community forums. They are defined by the voluntary engagement of people with diverse viewpoints in a sustained conversation over the social, economic, and environmental values of a particular place—a watershed, river basin, ecosystem, or rural community. It's hard to find a community or bioregion that does not have some type of study group, community forum, or citizen council. These forums clearly provide citizens something they are not getting through more formal, traditional opportunities for public participation and demonstrate, at least in part, that citizens are not apathetic, they simply want opportunities to be meaningfully involved in public decision making.

A number of organizations and institutions have emerged to support these policies and practices. At least seven states west of the 100th meridian have created some type of program or state office of dispute resolution and consensus building that specializes in natural resources and public policy.[25] Congress created the U.S. Institute for Environmental Conflict Resolution in 1998 to promote alternative dispute resolution on issues involving the federal government.[26] In Canada, every province has a Roundtable on the Economy and the Environment to seek agreement on strategies for sustainable development.[27]

Based on these trends, the opportunities to improve public participation in the twenty-first century seem to be nearly endless. We have the ideas, an emerging set of institutions, and an increasingly willing citizenry. The primary challenge, it seems, is that old habits are hard to break. Public officials are often skeptical about more inclusive, transparent public participation processes. Their willingness and ability to engage in collaborative processes are colored by the history of relationships with other stakeholders, which are often characterized by mistrust and misunderstanding. Public officials often lack experience with collaborative problem solving and are unfamiliar with how to integrate it into existing public participation and decision-making protocols. Federal officials often cite inflexible policies and procedures, particularly the Federal Advisory Committee Act.[28] They raise concerns about increasing the visibility of the problem, generating more controversy, creating expectations that cannot be met, abdicating their decision-making responsibility, and compromising their ability to make science-based decisions.

While most of these concerns raise practical issues that might be addressed through education and demonstration or pilot projects, Daniel Yankelovich, in *The Magic of Dialogue*, suggests that public officials resist meaningful public dialogue for two reasons.[29] One is a fear of losing status by sharing the power of policymaking with citizens. The second is the assumption that citizens are so ill informed, narrowly self-interested, unrealistic, and moralistic that they cannot add anything of value to the decision-making process. Even if Yankelovich's claims are only partially true, they help explain the inertia of public institutions.

Scholars, practitioners, and citizens need to be patient, yet persistent. Changing the culture of public decision making will not happen overnight. We can begin by encouraging and supporting leaders and champions within government and by documenting successful public participation in case studies.

We should also recognize and promote the broader, richer set of ideas available for engaging citizens. And most important, we can help citizens and officials learn to match the process to the situation so that these tools and strategies are not used inappropriately.

In addition to improving the process of public participation within existing systems of public decision making, it is also important to envision new, participatory systems of governance[30] and to provide the necessary skills for tomorrow's leaders and environmental decision makers. In some arenas, this is already happening. Fifteen professional natural resource schools in the United States now offer specific courses on public involvement, collaborative problem solving, and public dispute resolution—compared to only three in 1992.[31] Clearly, however, developing a more participatory culture for environmental decision making will be a lengthy process, requiring perseverance, creativity, and guarded optimism.

## Notes

1. U.S. Public Law 910190; 42 U.S.C. 4321–4347, Jan. 1, 1970. For a comprehensive assessment of NEPA, see Caldwell, L. K. *The National Environmental Policy Act: An Agenda for the Future.* Bloomington: Indiana University Press, 1998. Caldwell was one of the primary authors of the law.

2. For a summary of state environmental policy acts, see Mandelker, D. R. *NEPA Law and Litigation* (2nd ed.). St. Paul, Minn.: West, 1999; and Caldwell, L. K. "Beyond NEPA: Future Significance of the National Environmental Policy Act." *Harvard Environmental Law Review,* 1998, 22(1), 227. In short, following the enactment of NEPA in 1969 and as of 1999, fifteen states, the District of Columbia, and the Commonwealth of Puerto Rico have adopted state environmental policy acts that are generally modeled after NEPA. Other states have enacted specific statutes requiring environmental reviews of specific activities or activities in specific areas.

3. For an excellent list of tools, techniques, and strategies for public participation, see International Association for Public Participation. *Public Participation Toolbox.* [www.iap2.org]. See also Natural Resources Law Center, *Innovations in Forestry: Public Participation in Forest Planning.* Boulder, Colo.: University of Colorado School of Law, 1999; Jefferson Center. *Public Participation Workshop: Tools, Strategies, and Resources.* Minneapolis, Minn.: Jefferson Center, 2000; and Potapchuk, W. R. "New Approaches to Citizen Participation: Building Consent." *National Civic Review,* Spring 1991, 80, 158–168.

4. For one of the few evaluations of public participation under NEPA, see O'Connor Center for the Rocky Mountain West and Institute for Environment and Natural Resources. *Reclaiming NEPA's Potential: Can Collaborative Processes Improve Environmental Decision Making?* Missoula, Mont.: O'Connor Center for the Rocky Mountain West and Institute for Environment and Natural Resources, Mar. 2000. Also see Council on Environmental Quality, Executive Office of the President. *The National Environmental Policy Act: A Study of Its Effectiveness After Twenty-Five Years.* Washington, D.C.: Council on Environmental Quality, 1997. Even in Caldwell (1998) mediation is mentioned for resolving disputes after NEPA decisions are made, but there is no discussion of the effectiveness of public participation.

5. Montana Code Annotated 75-1-101; Montana Environmental Policy Act.

6. Senate Joint Resolution No. 18, A Joint Resolution of the Senate and the House of Representatives of the State of Montana Requesting that the Environmental Quality Council Conduct an Interim Study of the Montana Environmental Policy Act (1999).

7. This observation seems to be consistent with the work of John Sinclair and Alan Diduck, "Public Education: An Undervalued Component of the Environmental Assessment Public Involvement Process." *Environmental Impact Assessment Review,* 1995, *15,* 219–240.

8. Legislative Environmental Quality Council. *Improving the Montana Environmental Policy Act (MEPA) Process: Senate Joint Resolution No. 18.* Final Report to the 57th Legislature of the State of Montana, Nov. 2000.

9. See International Association for Public Participation. [www.iap2.org].

10. Glass, J. J. "Citizen Participation in Planning: The Relationship Between Objectives and Techniques." *American Planning Association Journal,* Apr. 1979, pp. 180–189.

11. The list was adapted from Jefferson Center (2000); and International Association for Public Participation. "Public Participation Spectrum." *Participation Quarterly,* 2000, *3,* 13.

12. Legislative Environmental Quality Council (2000).

13. See, for example, Wondelleck, J. *Public Lands Conflict and Resolution.* New York: Plenum, 1988.

14. Bolle, A. "Public Participation and Environmental Quality." *Natural Resources Journal,* July 1971, *11,* 497–505. One approach to achieve these objectives, albeit indirectly, is to encourage citizens and nongovernment organizations to convene their own public participation activities in addition to those formal activities initiated by public officials. For more on this strategy, see Richardson, T., Dusik, J., and Jindrova, P. "Parallel Public Participation: An Answer to Inertia in Decision-Making." *Environmental Impact Assessment Review,* 1998, *18,* 201–216.

15. The most comprehensive book available on consensus-based approaches to public decision making is Susskind, L., and others. *The Consensus Building Handbook.* Thousand Oaks, Calif.: Sage, 1999.

16. One recent articulation of the principles of deliberative democracy is Fung, A., and Wright, E. O. "Deepening Democracy: Innovations in Empowered Participatory Governance." Manuscript prepared for *Politics and Society,* Sept. 27, 2000. A slightly different approach to deliberative democracy is citizens juries. See Crosby, N. "Using the Citizens Jury Process for Environmental Decision Making." In K. Sexton and others (eds.), *Better Environmental Decisions: Strategies for Governments, Business, and Communities.* Washington, D.C.: Island Press, 1999, pp. 401–418.

17. Chrislip, D., and Larson, C. E. *Collaborative Leadership: How Citizens and Civic Leaders Can Make a Difference.* San Francisco: Jossey-Bass, 1994.

18. Burchfield, J. "Abandoned by the Roadside: The Long Road Ahead for Collaborative Stewardship." *Chronicle of Community,* 1998, 3(1), 31–36.

19. See *EPA Draft 2000 Public Involvement Policy.* [www.epa.gov/stakeholders/policy.html].

20. See McKinney, M. "Negotiated Rulemaking: Involving Citizens in Public Decisions." *Montana Law Review,* Summer 1999.

21. See Western Governors' Association Policy Resolution 97-024 on Consensus Building (Dec. 5, 1997); and Policy Resolution 99-013 on Principles for Environmental Management in the West (June 15, 1999). [www.westgov.org].

22. Council of State Governments-West, Western Municipal Conference, and Western Interstate Region, National Association of Counties. *The Role of Collaborative Problem Solving in Western Natural Resources: A Joint Policy Resolution.* Dec. 8, 2000.

23. Carlson, C. *Executive Orders: How Governors can Promote Collaborative Processes and Dispute Resolution for More Effective Governance.* Solutions to Establishing Sound Government DR Practices. Santa Fe, N.M.: Policy Consensus Initiative, Sept. 2000.

24. For a good introduction to these experiments in grassroots democracy, see Kenney, D., and others. *The New Watershed Sourcebook.* Boulder, Colo.: University of Colorado School of Law, Natural Resources Law Center, 2000.

25. The following organizations are connected in some way to state government. Some of them receive at least a portion of their funding from the state's general fund: Resource Solutions, University of Alaska; Udall Center for Public Policy, University of Arizona; Common Ground, University of California; Montana Consensus Council, Office of the Governor; Oregon

Dispute Resolution Commission; Texas Center for Public Policy Dispute Resolution, University of Texas; and the Institute for Environment and Natural Resources, University of Wyoming.

26. U.S. Public Law 105-156 (1998); also see www.ecr.gov

27. Cormick, G., Dale, N., Emond, P., Sigurdson, S. G., and Stuart, B. D. *Building Consensus for a Sustainable Future: Putting Principles into Action.* Ottawa: National Round Table on the Environment and the Economy, 1996.

28. 5 U.S.C. app. 2, secs. 1–15; see also 41 C.F.R., 101-6 and 102-3.

29. Yankelovich, D. *The Magic of Dialogue: Transforming Conflict into Cooperation.* New York: Simon & Schuster, 1999.

30. For one of the more provocative proposals for new systems of governance, see Kemmis, D. "A Democracy to Match Its Landscape." In R. B. Keiter (ed.), *Reclaiming the Native Home of Hope: Community, Ecology, and the American West.* Salt Lake City: University of Utah Press, 1998.

31. Harmon, W., McKinney, M., and Burchfield, J. "Public Involvement and Dispute Resolution Courses in Natural Resources Schools: A Five-Year Snapshot of Progress." *Journal of Forestry,* Sept. 1999.

*Matthew McKinney is executive director of the Montana Consensus Council, a public agency, and the Western Consensus Council, an independent, not-for-profit corporation.*

*Will Harmon is communications coordinator for the Montana Consensus Council and the Western Consensus Council.*

# Trends in Philanthropy: Democracy as Homeland Security

*David Mathews*

The war on terrorism, like all wars, challenges democracy. Crises put enormous pressure on representative government to make sound decisions and carry them out effectively. They test the values of democracy, as seen in the tension between security and the protection of civil liberties. Crises can also divert resources from domestic to international problems.

The relationship between philanthropy and democracy goes deeper, however, than September 11 and the war on terrorism. Foundations have an obligation to the political system that nourishes them. Our philanthropic institutions are a product of a particular brand of democracy that has prized self-rule and collective civic action. Some can trace their progress back to the Tocquevillian associations that flourished in an era when democracy was particularly robust, the early nineteenth century.

Our laws make it clear that we expect philanthropic institutions and other nongovernmental organizations (NGOs) to act on that obligation; throughout our history legislative bodies have chartered small groups of citizens to act in the larger public interest throughout history. These organizations are routinely asked to perform tasks in the interest of all. We have seen this in the recent devolution of responsibility for domestic problems from the federal to the state and community levels. Of course, some local foundations worry that too much is expected of them, but that is a separate issue.

## Democracy as Self-Rule Expressed in Collective Action

Some foundations are trying to meet their responsibilities more effectively by strengthening the underpinnings of democracy. But before I can explain what they are doing, I have to explain how I understand *democracy*. The word can refer to a system of government, to a way of life and a set of political values, or to self-rule carried out through the collective action of citizens. I think of self-rule as democracy at its most basic—rule by a sovereign people. I also

*Note:* This article is adapted from a lecture the author gave at the Waldemar A. Nielsen Issues in Philanthropy Lecture Series at Georgetown University on February 1, 2002.

believe that the public, like any sovereign, has to do more than consent to the actions of its representatives in government, who are the public's agents. The public has to be able to act on its own; it has to have the capacity to do common work.

In my own research, I've found any number of historical illustrations of this sovereign citizenry doing what Harry Boyte and Nan Kari call "public work."[1] The first half of the nineteenth century is filled with examples of people joining forces to build forts, maintain roads, and organize militias. It was a time, Robert Wiebe explains, when thousands spurred other thousands to action.[2]

I am not suggesting that the early 1800s were the good old days of democracy. Yet citizens appear to have had a sense of what they could accomplish together, and they created a muscular, sweaty public through common work. Nineteenth-century Americans weren't civic saints; most probably weren't motivated by noble ideals like sacrifice for the common good. Yet, as Alexis de Tocqueville observed, they had an appreciation for the interrelatedness of their separate concerns, which he characterized as self-interests rightly or well understood. Americans, he pointed out, "almost always know how to combine their own well-being" with the well-being of others. This doesn't require people to make the interests of others their own or to contribute unselfishly for the benefit of all. It just means that citizens have to see the relationship between their concerns and those of others. That was possible in early America, even though people sometimes abandoned themselves to what Tocqueville described as "the disinterested and unreflective sparks that are natural to man."[3]

Nineteenth-century Americans did public work for and through communities. Turning frontier settlements into civilized space where a valued way of life could take hold was a major industry in these formative years. As John Dewey reminds us, "American democratic polity was developed out of genuine community life," in which people can experience democracy directly and personally. Dewey goes on to argue that "unless local community life can be restored, the public cannot resolve its most urgent problem: to find and identify itself."[4]

Dewey identified a central problem in modern democracy that should concern foundations: the "eclipse of the public."[5] After September 11, we were all inspired by the citizens of New York, who demonstrated that common work is still possible—and still necessary. But the response of New Yorkers to the crisis must be seen against the backdrop of people's uncertainty about the role of a supposedly sovereign public. Months after the attacks, Americans are still asking, "What can we do?" We aren't sure about our capacity for collective action or how effective it will be. This uncertainty is particularly evident among our young people. As Bill Galston points out, they are willing to volunteer for personal acts of charity (perhaps because they can see immediate results) but lack confidence in common action.[6] A recent survey by Robert Putnam shows we are more trusting of government and our neighbors since September 11.

Yet impulses like greater charitable giving played out in a matter of weeks. It remains to be seen whether shifts in attitudes just after the attacks will translate into more civic activism.[7]

The prevailing lack of confidence in the power of citizens is curious, given that self-rule has had such a rich history. After all, a community-based public gave us much of what we have today: the country itself (through Revolutionary War militias), our public schools (through township and district school boards), and even some of our businesses (such as the first railroad companies, which were organized through town meetings). Part of the problem may be that many citizens believe the institutions they created to help them in civic action still work *for* them, but no longer know how to work *with* them. Public schools, for instance, are often seen as difficult to reach and too bureaucratized to be effective partners.

Another reason Americans may be less confident in themselves is their feeling that citizens don't have what it takes to affect a now global world. Since the shock of World War I and the recognition that conflict can spread around the planet like a fire out of control, Walter Lippmann and others (including John Dewey) have argued that we are subject to forces so vast, so complex, and so indirect in their consequences that average citizens cannot possibly understand what is happening.[8]

## The Civil Investing Initiative

The concept of American democracy as community based but not community limited, as well as the idea that democracy is rooted in self-responsibility, self-rule, and collective action, informs the work of many foundations. Bruce Sievers, former president of the Walter and Elise Haas Fund, has already illustrated a sensitivity to this understanding of democracy in his critique of venture philanthropy, which he spelled out in a paper presented in the Nielsen seminars at Georgetown University.[9] Sievers and other philanthropists who question some of the sacred assumptions of their field began to share their concerns around 1994. Anna Faith Jones (then at the Boston Foundation and later chair of the Council on Foundations) set the tone of the conversations with her candid admission that some of her organization's grantmaking had not always been effective, even after seventy-five years of investing. (Her comment was especially significant because the Boston Foundation is one of the best in the country.) Her point was that it was time to rethink not only grantmaking but also the role of philanthropy. Those who felt this same unease began to ask what the alternatives might be. Some participants in the discussion with Sievers and Jones were from community foundations, some were from smaller national foundations started by businesses, and some (though not as many) were from large grantmakers. The Kettering Foundation has kept records of the meetings and has provided relevant research.[10]

The objective of this group of foundations has been to get at the problems behind the problems; that is, to address structural or systemic barriers to self-determination and effective civic action. The meetings have focused on what must be in place in communities *before* program grants can be successful. After a few years, enough experiments were under way that these initiatives (called *civil investing*) were featured in both *The Chronicle of Philanthropy* and *Foundation News & Commentary.* The most recent meeting of the group was held last year in Chicago.

## Wicked Problems and Political Will

My own view is that the civil investing initiative has been stimulated by pressure from "wicked" problems, problems that won't go away because they are deeply embedded in society. Racial discrimination and poverty are examples. Combating them requires a large amount of ongoing political will—a commodity that philanthropies cannot buy or rent, even with all of their resources. Furthermore, wicked problems require a response from the community as a whole. A single institution or segment of the population is not likely to be effective. These problems also need the attention of an engaged public, as opposed to a persuaded population. When people have been persuaded by leaders or sold on some master plan (whatever its merits), they do not usually have sufficient ownership to generate the necessary political will.

Ronald Heifetz, a professor of government at Harvard University who trained as a physician, has a deep appreciation of the distinctive characteristics of wicked problems. It is not surprising that he bases his argument for an engaged public on his experience with medical conditions that are also wicked. In Heifetz's typology, health problems range from mechanical difficulties, which can be remedied by a physician (such as a broken arm), to the more serious ones, for which there are no technical fixes (such as diabetes). For the latter the patient and physician have to combine forces. The same is true of our most serious political problems—those that governments and professionals, with all their competence, cannot handle by themselves.[11]

Two scholars, Horst Rittel and Melvin Webber, call problems wicked when (1) the diagnosis or definition is unclear, (2) the location or cause is uncertain, and (3) any effective action to deal with them requires narrowing "the gap between what-is and what-ought-to-be" while there is disagreement about the latter.[12]

Conventional ways of responding to problems are ill-suited to those that are wicked. Most problem-solving strategies are based on our national experience in dealing with the difficulties of post–Great Depression America. Many of those were discrete and definable; they could be addressed by setting concrete goals and eradicated through the application of professional expertise. Though by no means easy to solve, these problems did have solutions. In this sense, they were "tame." After the Depression, professionals designed programs to build affordable housing, clean the water supply, construct schools and hospitals, and stabilize financial institutions. They went on to create a national highway system and to treat what had been untreatable diseases. Their programs were successful, so their methods of analyzing, planning, and evaluating were adopted by governments and nongovernmental institutions alike.

Wicked problems, however, are neither discrete nor easily defined. They are as tricky as they are aggressive and vicious. Each is a symptom of another, in a never-ending chain. While bridges can be built and diseases held at bay, wicked problems persist. Success cannot be determined in the same way as the reliability of an engineered structure or the curative power of a laboratory-developed drug. A shared understanding of the approximate nature of what people are facing is crucial. Dealing effectively with a wicked problem may depend on *not* reaching a fixed decision about a solution early on. Retaining the ability to explore several options and experiment is more important.

Take the persistence of poverty in the face of rising prosperity. Why should the homeless population have continued to grow while per capita income increased significantly at the end of the last century? What is the real problem? And what causes it? Is poverty the absence of resources, of education, of personal motivation? The debate is endless. Where is the source of poverty? Is it the economic system, or is it a social subculture? Will there be an end to it, or will the poor be always with us? Could we ever agree on an acceptable level of poverty?

To the extent that foundation operating procedures are based on the conventional means of addressing so-called tame problems, they are subject to challenge. Accordingly, the civil investing discussions have questioned old assumptions.

## The Mystery of the Space in Between: Remapping Political Society

My interpretation of what motivated the civil investing group is only that—my interpretation. Actually, few participants in the discussions have based their conclusions on scholarly literature. Most have been convinced by their own experiences that they are facing intractable problems requiring a more engaged citizenry.

Foundation folks are practical. Those in the civil investing group want to focus on what can be done about problems that frustrate everyone. Fresh insights have come from identifying structures and practices that have not been fully utilized in addressing persistent, systemic problems. These insights were captured in a series of charts made during the meetings. Figure 1 is a picture of political life consisting of a private world of individuals and a public world of governments.

Participants saw immediately that the chart was misleading—something was missing. They said that there was a space between individuals and governments, though not everyone could agree on its name. Some referred to it as "public space," others said "public life," and still others thought of it as "community." Several people used a phrase that was being revived just as the group began its work; they said the space was occupied by the "civil society," or the society that citizens create with other citizens. (See Figure 2.)

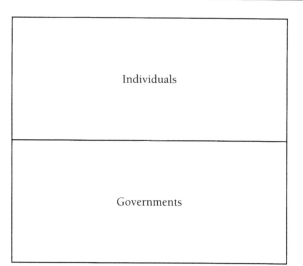

Figure 1.  Chart One.

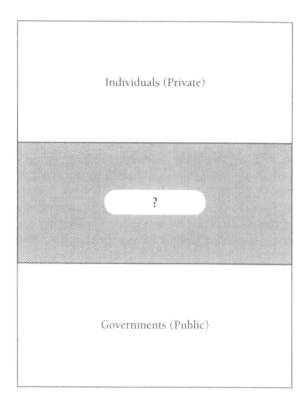

Figure 2.  Chart Two.

The group quickly realized that the top and bottom segments were not the same size, because there are more individuals than governments. So the rectangle became an inverted triangle, with people at the top and governments at the bottom.

The group also identified two types of organizations they saw in the space in the middle. Some were nongovernmental institutions; others were informal, ad hoc associations. So in the third chart (Figure 3), NGOs were represented by squares, and the less formal, ad hoc groups by circles and later as mushy clouds, intended to reflect their unstructured, often temporary character.

This chart prompted a discussion of whether foundations can deal indirectly with ad hoc groups—through formal NGOs—or whether they have to

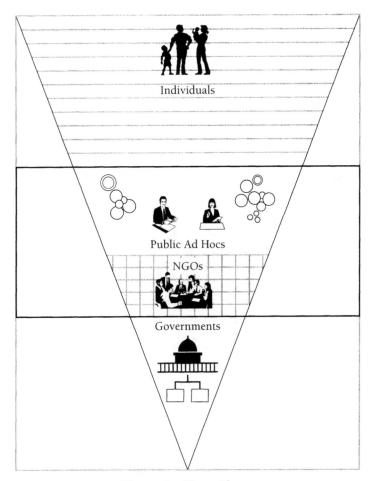

**Figure 3. Chart Three.**

work more closely with the loosely structured associations because these organizations might respond more effectively to wicked problems.

The fourth chart captures a sobering insight. Foundations, along with other NGOs, like to think of themselves as allied with citizens and as decidedly not governmental. Citizens, however, often feel that many NGOs are similar to government agencies. And when people's attitude toward government is negative, they are inclined to tar civic organizations with the same brush. The realization of this disconnect was represented by a heavy jagged line and placed, not between the public sector and the government, but between the informal and formal institutions of public life. (See Figure 4.)

Foundations that wanted to cross the divide ran into barriers. For example, how could they fund citizens associations, even those that had

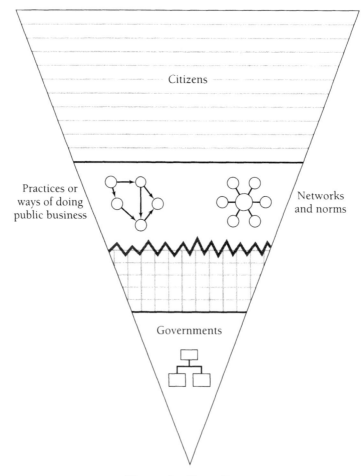

**Figure 4.  Chart Four.**

demonstrated that they could drive drug dealers out of neighborhoods, if they didn't have 501(c)(3) status?

Despite such obstacles, those participating in the civil investing seminars see the space between individuals and governments as the area where their organizations have to become more active. That conclusion has led them to look even more closely at what occupies this space. They have sometimes focused on structures, networks, and norms. (Robert Putnam's findings about "bowling alone" had just been published when the group started meeting and doubtlessly influenced this view.[13]) At other times, foundations have seen the space between as a dynamic arena of action and interaction. They have turned their attention to group behaviors, processes, and ways of doing civic business, which the Kettering Foundation calls "practices." This wasn't an either-or discussion; no one thought that practices exist apart from norms and structures or that structures and norms exist apart from practices.

Another conversation developed around the question of whether everything that happens in the space between citizens and governments is positive. Some said that even if the space is a civil society, it is not necessarily civil. They see citizens increasingly organizing around identities and convictions that cannot be mediated, and warn that conflict is inevitable. New organizations were emerging that critics called NOPEs (Not on Planet Earth) and CAVEs (Citizens Against Virtually Everything).

## Democratic Practices That Address Wicked Problems

While appreciating the importance of networks and norms, Kettering research set out to identify practices that could generate "public capital," the foundation's term for a more explicitly political form of social capital.

Recall that problems are considered wicked when there is no shared sense of their names or their causes. People will disagree morally over what should be done about them. Wicked problems require the exercise of sound judgment about the nature of the difficulty and the most appropriate response. That in turn requires deliberation—the kind of talking and reasoning used to guide action when people differ on both means and ends.

Kettering has been studying deliberation for more than twenty years. Deliberation isn't casual discussion or partisan debate. Simply put, it is weighing the costs and consequences of various options for action against all the things that are most valuable to us.[14] We all deliberate privately, alone or with our friends, as when we decide on a career move. Public deliberations typically begin in a coffee shop or at dinner, and they may continue at a town meeting. The result is seldom a clear-cut decision or consensus as in private life, when only a few are involved. In observing deliberative forums, the Kettering Foundation has found that people are more likely to identify a broad direction for action or decide what they will and will not do in order to solve a problem. As they struggle with the options, they often come to a new understanding of the problem, one that incorporates various dimensions of the problem as a variety of people experience it.

During the last few years, some scholars have argued that deliberation is indispensable to democracy. Political theorists such as Amy Gutmann, Dennis Thompson, and James Fishkin treat deliberation as synonymous with democracy because it recognizes that most political decisions are, in fact, normative and have, as the ancient Greeks said, more than one answer.[15]

Deliberation seems capable of generating the political will required to combat wicked problems and to energize, if not an entire community, multiple political actors. Public will is strongest when citizens meet face-to-face to redefine problems in their own terms, exchange opinions, and fashion workable arrangements for action. A citizenry that makes up its own mind is likely to end up with sustainable commitments, as opposed to short bursts of enthusiasm. As I suggested earlier, the commitments of a persuaded populace might not have that kind of staying power. Deliberating generates political energy by promoting ownership. It is just common sense that we tend to take more responsibility for what we participate in deciding than we do for what others decide for us.

Redefining problems through deliberation may also prompt people to see ways of responding that were not apparent before, broadening the range of potential actors. And the shared sense of direction that can result from deliberation promotes complementary initiatives, making the whole of a civic enterprise greater than the sum of its parts.

Kettering research has identified two other democratic practices that precede decision making. One is as simple as the way problems are named. The other is how the terms of the public conversation are determined, or the way issues are framed.[16]

Naming an issue is critical because the public often has a different take on an issue from that of professionals and institutions. For example, citizens are inclined to see stopping drug abuse as a personal and family concern rather than as a matter of law enforcement or of preventing drugs from coming into the country. The name we give a problem determines who will be available to deal with it and what kind of response will emerge. Finding out how the public sees an issue is, therefore, crucial to finding out how citizens can get their hands on elusive difficulties that defy the best grant programs.

Once a problem is given a name that captures the different ways people experience it, it has to be framed for discussion. Issues are sometimes presented as a contest between opposing camps polarized around conflicting ideologies—there are only two options. In other situations, a community might consider three or four options, each presented as fairly as possible and with information on the pros and cons. (This, by the way, is how the National Issues Forums briefing books are framed.[17]) These differences in framings play out in the ways communities tackle their problems. When issues are polarized from the beginning, the chances of success are minimal.

## Unfinished Business: Challenges to Civil Investing

This report on the civil investing initiative would not be complete without discussing the obstacles. Whether foundations want to strengthen networks or encourage democratic practices, they face practical challenges. For what and to whom should they award grants? If barbecues and choral groups are characteristic of a strong civil society, should funds go for pigs and sheet music? Or should people be paid to deliberate? Doing what seems to be the obvious has had unintended consequences. When citizens were paid to talk to one another in one impoverished country, they became less willing to deliberate without a stipend.

## Evaluation and Civic Learning

Foundations have found evaluation of their civil investments especially daunting. We insist on knowing results because we want to be successful—as well we should. If we did not, efforts to strengthen public life would degenerate into the worst kind of therapy: providing warm but illusory feelings of momentary comfort. Outcomes must be known and evident to more than those directly involved. But conventional evaluation may be counterproductive and limit understanding of the subtleties and intangibles that play a role in civic renewal. A study done for Kettering by the Harwood Group shows that some evaluations legitimize only those actions that lead to easily quantifiable results.[18] Even more serious, traditional ways of assessing outcomes may undermine the very thing that makes for long-term success—civic learning.

Civic learning is closely associated with democracy and is a corollary of collective action. It prompts people to keep on acting. This form of collective learning allows us to know those things about our communities that we can know only by talking together. That includes what is truly valuable to us as a community, what our interrelated interests are, whether we have compatible purposes, and what we should do in responding to common problems. People do not discover many of these things, rather they create them through the kind of talk people use to teach themselves before they act.

Civic learning can be stymied when measuring success is reduced to setting goals or establishing benchmarks and measuring outcomes, particularly if the assessment is done only by outsiders.[19] In order to evaluate the worth of actions, people have to look at what happened and simultaneously at the effects on what they consider valuable. Two determinations are required. Asking only what outcomes can be identified isn't enough. We have to revisit—continually revisit—the prior question of what outcomes we want. Our notion of desirable consequences usually changes as we act.

I believe we need a kind of evaluation that is compatible with democracy, one that looks at *who* needs to know the results as well as *how* the results are known. Democracy-friendly evaluation has as its criterion a greater capacity for self-rule or self-determination. The indications of that capacity are collective decision making and collective action, as well as the public space (or opportunities) for such practices.

Evaluating civil investments is particularly difficult because there probably aren't any models of excellence or best practices to use as standards. Civic learning is experimental and innovative rather than imitative. ("Imitation is limitation," some communities have told us.[20]) This kind of learning is essential in a democracy because we don't have (and won't accept) any authority to give us answers. We have to figure things out for ourselves, and we do this largely by trial and error.

Foundations (and other NGOs) need to encourage civic innovation. Their willingness to do this in times of crisis is particularly crucial, not only in communities but also in governments. Even in normal circumstances, governments tend to lock onto one-size-fits-all solutions to complex social problems. Partisan politics take over. Proposed solutions are cloaked in moral certainty, although no one can be sure the remedies will be effective. Few are willing to look for alternatives.

Foundations have a long history of stimulating change. But they must continue to have environments where they "learn to fail intelligently." That, Charles Kettering said, is the secret of invention.

Perhaps there is a role here at the university centers for the study of philanthropy, which Virginia Hodgkinson and Independent Sector helped establish. Foundations themselves need space to do their own experimenting and learning. I got this idea from watching the civil investing group. I saw foundation officers take their standard operating procedures in one hand and their understanding of how democracy works in the other, and then imagine what they could do to make the two fit more closely. At a meeting in Miami, someone asked what we think democracy requires. The response was community self-determination. With that definition in mind, someone else suggested looking at how foundations decide on grant programs, select criteria for proposals, and assess results. Most of these standard operating procedures did not appear to be fully consistent with democratic self-rule. At the same time, foundation officers did not think they could simply give their funds to communities to use as they saw fit. Such anomalies are opportunities for experimentation.

Despite all the difficulties associated with learning to fail successfully, social experimentation and the collective learning that must go with it are essential to the vitality of our democracy. And the strength of our democracy is the ultimate in homeland security.

### Notes

1 For more on public work, see Boyte, H. C., and Kari, N. N. *Building America: The Democratic Promise of Public Work*. Philadelphia: Temple University Press, 1996. The results of my search for the historical public will appear in *Why Public Schools? Whose Public Schools?*

*Stories from Early Alabama,* forthcoming.

2. Wiebe, R. H. *Self-Rule: A Cultural History of American Democracy.* Chicago: University of Chicago Press, 1995, p. 71.

3. Tocqueville, A. de. *Democracy in America,* trans. H. C. Mansfield and D. Winthrop. Chicago: University of Chicago Press, 2000, pp. 359, 501–502.

4. Dewey, J. *The Public and Its Problems.* Chicago: Swallow Press, 1954, pp. 111, 216.

5. Dewey (1954), p. 110.

6. Galston, W. A. "Can Patriotism Be Turned into Civic Engagement?" *Chronicle of Higher Education,* Nov. 16, 2001, p. B16.

7. Putnam, R. "Bowling Together," *American Prospect,* Feb. 11, 2002, 13.

8. Lippmann, W. *The Phantom Public.* New York: Harcourt, Brace, 1925.

9. Sievers, B. "If Pigs Had Wings: The Appeals and Limits of Venture Philanthropy." Speech presented at the Waldemar A. Nielsen Issues in Philanthropy Lecture Series, Georgetown University, Nov. 16, 2001.

10. "Learning About Civil Society: A Graphic Record of the Civil Investing Seminars" (rev. ed.). Dayton, Ohio: Kettering Foundation, Oct. 1999, photocopy.

11. Ronald Heifetz and Riley Sinder make this analogy in "Political Leadership: Managing the Public's Problem Solving." In Robert B. Reich (ed.), *The Power of Public Ideas.* Cambridge, Mass.: Ballinger, 1988.

12. Rittel, H.W.J., and Webber, M. J. "Dilemmas in a General Theory of Planning." *Policy Sciences,* 1973, *4,* 155–169.

13. See Putnam, R. D. "Bowling Alone: America's Declining Social Capital." *Journal of Democracy,* 1995, *6,* 65–78. Putnam later wrote a book on this subject: *Bowling Alone: The Collapse and Revival of American Community.* New York: Simon & Schuster, 2000.

14. For a more extensive account of what Kettering has learned from deliberative forums, see Mathews, D. *Politics for People: Finding a Responsible Public Voice* (2nd ed.). Urbana: University of Illinois Press, 1999, chap. 12 ("The Power of Choice").

15. Gutmann, A., and Thompson, D. *Democracy and Disagreement.* Cambridge, Mass.: Harvard University Press, 1996; Fishkin, J. S. *Democracy and Deliberation: New Directions for Democratic Reform.* New Haven, Conn.: Yale University Press, 1991.

16. A Kettering working paper, "For Communities to Work," describes democratic practices in some detail.

17. For an account of the National Issues Forums, see Sirianni, C., and Friedland, L. *Civic Innovation in America: Community Empowerment, Public Policy, and the Movement for Civic Renewal.* Berkeley: University of California Press, 2001.

18. Harwood Group. *Squaring Realities: Governing Boards and Community-Building.* Dayton, Ohio: Kettering Foundation, Aug. 2000, p. 20.

19. Frederickson, H. G. *Best Practice, Benchmarking and Cheating Innovation.* Dayton, Ohio: Kettering Foundation, May 2000.

20. For a detailed portrait of community learning, see Grisham, V. L., Jr. *Tupelo: The Evolution of a Community.* Dayton, Ohio: Kettering Foundation Press, 1999.

*David Mathews is president of the Kettering Foundation.*

# Changing Channels: How the Nonprofit Sector Can Help Improve Local Television News

*Sean P. Treglia*

As the primary source of political information for most Americans, local news plays a critical role in our democracy.[1] As the quality of local news has declined over the last two decades, serious concerns have been raised about the potential consequences for civil society. To improve programming, a number of civic groups, scholars, and foundations are calling on the federal government to increase its enforcement of the news media's long-standing public interest obligations. Success in these efforts is far from certain, however, because the once-friendly regulatory environment has all but unraveled in recent years. While the struggle to strengthen the media's public interest obligations should continue, what is needed is a complementary approach that balances the stick of government regulation with the carrot of the free market. Working with broadcasters, the nonprofit sector can help improve the quality of news by making the case that such coverage can be profitable.

## The Rise and Decline of Public Interest Obligations in Broadcast Media

The very first battle over broadcast airwaves took place off the coast of North Carolina during World War I. The U.S. Navy wanted the airwaves free for military communications, pitting it against private individuals who were talking with each other via home radios. The federal government settled the dispute (on behalf of the military), but soon after the war two competing visions for use of the airwaves emerged. Public groups such as churches, schools, and civic organizations believed the airwaves were public property that should be regulated to ensure they were used for the enrichment of democracy. Private companies believed that government regulation should be limited and that regulations developed should focus on helping to develop and support the commercial media. The struggle between these competing visions has defined government policy toward the electronic media ever since.

In the era of activist government of the 1930s, Congress passed a series of laws resolving (for a time) this dispute. The analog spectrum[2] was deemed public property, but private companies could be licensed to use the airwaves for profit if they agreed to dedicate a specified amount of airtime to programming with a "public purpose." The novel compromise was based on the concept of scarcity. The analog spectrum was a valuable but finite public resource that would best benefit society if developed by the private sector. In return for the right to profit from use of the public's airwaves, however, private broadcasters were obligated to devote a certain amount of airtime and resources to the general betterment of democracy.

In its heyday the system of public interest obligations required local stations to provide such things as news updates once every hour; reduced rates for candidate advertisements; free airtime to local nonprofit organizations for public service announcements; public debate, by providing free airtime to local organizations to express opinions on important topics; and equal time for the expression of opposing views. The concept of scarcity of the analog spectrum, the assumption of public ownership of the airwaves, and the detailed arrangement of public interest obligations were challenged by broadcasters but found constitutional by the Supreme Court in a case commonly referred to as *Red Lion Broadcasting*.

The election of Ronald Reagan as president ushered in a more laissez-faire period in American politics, leading to the gradual dismantling of the public interest obligations regulatory framework. This antiregulation movement culminated when Congress passed the Telecommunications Act of 1996. The act was drafted due to the development of technology that enabled use of the digital spectrum[3] for broadcasting and other forms of communications. Broadcasters have been quick to point out that the digital spectrum (which can carry exponentially more broadcast signals than the analog spectrum) makes the concept of scarcity—and by implication public interest obligations—obsolete. In response, critics argue that even with the increase in channels offered by the digital spectrum, the public still owns the airwaves, scarcity still remains an issue, and there is no guarantee that private media organizations will voluntarily provide programming that serves the public interest. They contend that since *Red Lion Broadcasting* remains the law of the land, media organizations' public interest obligations should still exist and be enforced.

Despite the ongoing debate, in many ways the combination of technology, economics, and Congressional politics has already made the issue moot. The Telecommunications Act handed an important but little understood political victory to broadcasters. The act literally gave the digital spectrum (with an estimated value at the time of over $17 billion dollars) to commercial broadcasters. In exchange, broadcasters "committed" to an unspecified set of new public interest obligations to be determined by a presidential commission (the Gore Commission) made up of representatives of civic groups, the academic community, and the media industry. However, after months of contentious deliberation and after the digital spectrum was legally transferred to their possession, broadcasters refused to agree to any obligations under the act.

Local stations are investing substantial resources and will soon make the technological jump from analog to digital broadcasting. When that technological shift occurs *Red Lion Broadcasting* will no longer be controlling because the case applies to the analog and not the digital spectrum. Even though *Red Lion Broadcasting* has never been overturned by the Supreme Court and is still technically the law of the land, the Telecommunications Act focuses on the digital spectrum and not the analog spectrum, and when local stations go digital, the holding in *Red Lion Broadcasting*—as a matter of fact—simply will not apply. As a result, what little remains of the current set of public interest obligations will no longer apply. In addition, Congress has done little to renew the discussion of new public interest obligations under the Telecommunications Act since the failure of the Gore Commission, so no new obligations will be in effect after the technological shift occurs. In short, as a matter of law, local television stations will soon have no obligations for news that serves the public interest. The statutory requirement that broadcasters agree to a new set of obligations under the act remains, but the eventual outcome of the political fight to enforce that requirement is far from certain.

Even prior to this shift, the abandonment of public interest obligations by broadcasters has already had a disastrous effect on the quality of local news coverage of campaigns. Through the 1970s, the quality of news coverage was considered reasonably good, and television was generally perceived to exert healthy, unifying effects on the nation. But beginning in the 1980s and continuing through the most recent election, the quality of news coverage on commercial TV has declined by every conceivable measure. For example, according to a recent study by the Committee for the Study of the American Electorate, in ten battleground states only two of approximately 198 campaign debates were shown by local stations on prime time TV.[4] According to a report by the University of Southern California's Annenberg School for Communication, more television airtime is now devoted to political advertising than to news coverage of campaigns. And a recent, hotly contested gubernatorial race in California received less than nine seconds a night of news coverage from local stations in the final weeks of the campaign.

As the quantity of news coverage has shrunk, the quality has also diminished. According to a series of studies conducted by the Annenberg School for Communication at the University of Pennsylvania, what little campaign coverage remains is generally cast in cynical or highly sensationalistic frames. A review of news stories during the 2000 presidential primary race, for example, found that less than 13 percent addressed issues that would affect the public if any of the candidates were elected president. The remainder covered topics such as fund raising, strategy and tactics, and insider opinions. The studies referred to in this section were funded in part by The Pew Charitable Trusts.

## A New Approach to Improving the Quality
## of Local News

The fight to secure a new set of public interest obligations continues, led by groups such as the Alliance for Better Campaigns, the Media Access Project, the Consumers Union, and BetterTV.org. These and other groups have tirelessly promoted their cause to policy makers, generated coverage in the print media, built grassroots coalitions at the local level, lodged complaints with the FCC, and sponsored detailed research documenting that local broadcasters have all but abandoned public interest programming. As a result they have won several small but important political victories such as the Torricelli Amendment to the McCain-Feingold bill in the Senate[5] and the pledge by Senator McCain to introduce a so-called free airtime bill in Congress.[6] This legal and regulatory approach to establishing public interest obligations in the digital era is important and should continue. Given the economics of the media and the politics of the time, there is no guarantee of success, however, especially in the short run. In addition, as the experience of the 1980s and 1990s suggests, even if new laws and regulations are put in place there is no assurance that they will be followed or enforced in ways that will measurably improve the quality of local news.

One of the major roadblocks to improving the amount and quality of local news is that broadcasters are skeptical that serious campaign and political coverage is of interest to viewers. Doubts about the economic value of political news have driven the recent decline in coverage. They have also fueled the increasingly sensationalistic and cynical tone of coverage, because common wisdom among the media consultants who advise local stations is that only this kind of coverage will attract viewers. This assumption has never been adequately tested because there are few entities outside the commercial structure of the television industry that have the resources to produce and promote alternative approaches.

Ironically, local television news viewership has declined along with declining quality, raising serious doubts within the industry about the validity of media consultants' advice and opening the door for new and potentially more informative and useful forms of coverage. However, even if they are inclined to experiment with new formats, local stations are often unable to do so because of the economics of the news industry. The rise of cable, satellite, and Internet news sources has made it difficult for independent stations to stay afloat. The result has been the rapid consolidation of ownership of local stations by a handful of the media giants. In 1980, some fifty companies owned about half of all local stations. By 2000, less than ten companies owned almost two-thirds of all local broadcasters with a dozen smaller companies making up the balance. These large corporate owners seek to increase profits quickly, putting local stations under great pressure to generate revenues through their news operations.[7] To this end, over the last decade stations have been forced to reduce newsroom costs, seriously undermining their ability to cover local news. This point is not lost on reporters and producers, who are increasingly concerned about the quality of the product they deliver nightly to their viewers. But things are likely only to get worse, unless stations are able to find ways to improve coverage that will simultaneously maintain and increase audiences.

All these challenges have encouraged scholars to explore other ways to ensure that the public has access to high-quality local news and information. One influential scholar at the American Enterprise Institute has developed the radical idea of using public funding to build an alternative news source. Under this plan the digital spectrum would be auctioned off to the highest bidder with no strings attached. The money from this auction would be invested in the Public Broadcasting Service or another form of public broadcasting to ensure the long-term viability of an alternative source of quality news. Although this idea deserves serious consideration, it does not address the economic disparity and the wide gap in reach between public and commercial TV. Even with better funding for public television the need for commercial broadcasters to provide quality news will still exist.

A different and in many ways equally controversial idea is for the nonprofit sector to partner with commercial stations to design models of quality coverage and conduct market and viewer research on the economic and civic impact of such coverage that informs the development of business plans to help reorganize newsrooms into high-quality, commercially viable enterprises. This approach is based on the assumptions that (1) the only way to improve local news coverage is to invest more resources in news operations; (2) this will happen only if media owners are convinced they will see a return on this investment; and (3) properly designed and promoted news formats can be simultaneously informative, engaging, and profitable. But left to their own devices, commercial stations are unlikely to invest the resources necessary to adequately test these assumptions. Working with commercial stations, the nonprofit sector can provide the technical, intellectual, and financial start-up capital to develop and market test new formats, with the goal of demonstrating to broadcasters the journalistic and economic benefits of quality news coverage.

The idea of the nonprofit sector using its limited resources to help commercial media make a profit is bound to generate controversy. Nonetheless, it is already happening with early but encouraging results in the following projects funded in part by The Pew Charitable Trusts. In addition to its efforts in support of mandatory public interest obligations, the Alliance for Better Campaigns is spearheading a national effort to encourage local television stations to voluntarily adopt the "5/30 standard" (five minutes a night of quality campaign coverage during the thirty days prior to an election). The 5/30 standard was endorsed by several major networks and adopted by close to 10 percent of the nation's local stations during the 2000 presidential elections. Preliminary evidence suggests that there were improvements in the amount and quality of campaign coverage provided by these stations as compared to those not adopting the standard. The next step is to determine whether this improved coverage helped stations maintain or even increase their news audiences—a crucial issue if stations are to be convinced to continue in this vein.

One finding to emerge early during the Alliance for Better Campaigns' 5/30 initiative was that local television stations were often at a loss as to how to use the airtime effectively. With this in mind, the University of Southern California's Annenberg School for Communication assembled a series of videos of over 100 clips of quality news stories and formats from stations across the country. The clips were selected according to criteria designed by a team of scholars, news directors, and reporters, and they showcased campaign news formats that would both attract and inform viewers. The videos were circulated at professional conferences of news directors, producers, and reporters, through the USC Annenberg Web site, and via direct mail to news directors and reporters. Many of the formats showcased in the videos were adopted by local stations for their 2000 election coverage, and USC-Annenberg plans to continue and expand its efforts in the 2002 campaign.

A project led by Wisconsin Public Television takes a more hands-on approach by building partnerships between commercial and public stations in local television markets. (Thirteen partnerships were formed during the 2000 election, with plans to expand to thirty markets in 2002.) Public-private partners in each market pool resources, talent, and ideas, providing commercial stations with the resources and expertise to innovate and public stations with the skills to improve production techniques and increase their reach. The project offers training sessions for reporters on ways to improve their campaign coverage, conferences to share story and coverage ideas, a Web site with e-mail alerts to spread innovations, and sessions with station managers to make the case that quality news can increase their bottom line. As with the Alliance for Better Campaigns and the USC Annenberg initiatives, systematic evidence on the journalistic and economic impact of the Wisconsin Public Television project is needed. (Plans are in place to do this in 2002.) Preliminary evidence does suggest, however, that the quality of coverage by participating stations improved and that some of the new formats developed through the project were adopted by nonparticipating stations in the same or surrounding media markets.

Making the case to station managers that "quality sells" is key to the success of efforts such as those described above. While systematic evidence to make this case is largely lacking to date, and there is no guarantee that high-quality news will appeal to viewers, some support for this view has been documented by the nonprofit Project for Excellence in Journalism (PEJ). In a series of recent studies, PEJ looked at stations in a variety of market conditions and consistently found a direct correlation between high audience ratings for news and quality news programming. However, it also found that stations airing particularly sensationalistic, lowest-common-denominator news programming also attracted news viewers, and that producing high-quality news was more expensive than producing low-quality news. PEJ has been working to further describe the characteristics of quality television news and to offer advice to local stations on how to keep costs down while still producing such news.

Even as such projects work to improve the quality of local television news, it is important to keep abreast of trends in the industry that may provide new opportunities for change. The technologies that paved the way for digital broadcasting will also usher in the era of interactive TV that most experts agree is just around the corner. Interactive TV will resemble the Internet and enable viewers to learn more about topics that interest them by searching through layers of information while watching the nightly news. Although this technology offers the possibility of more in-depth, relevant news and information, there is no reason to automatically assume that this will be the case. Here again the nonprofit community can play a crucial role in providing commercial media with the models and evidence necessary to demonstrate how the use of the Internet can benefit citizens while attracting audiences. One effort to do this is under way at the Annenberg School for Communication at the University of Pennsylvania. Penn-Annenberg has conducted extensive research on best practices for the provision of useful, accessible, and engaging campaign information via the Internet, including how to present candidate biographies, issue positions, ad watches, and campaign finance information. Working with the Radio and Television News Directors Foundation, Penn-Annenberg will form partnerships with ten commercial broadcasters in the 2002 campaign to pilot these innovative formats on local stations' Web sites, and integrate and cross-promote them with the nightly broadcast news. As part of this experiment, Penn-Annenberg will conduct attitudinal and market research designed to learn whether quality information on local news Web sites can increase citizens' engagement in campaigns in a way that addresses broadcasters' need to maintain and increase audiences in a cost-effective manner.

There is no guarantee that projects such as those described here will succeed, and it will take carefully designed, objective data and research before a convincing case can be made to broadcasters that quality news is good journalism and good business. Legitimate concerns also have and will continue to be raised—from both the news media and the nonprofit sector—about the appropriateness of such private-public partnerships. However, those of us interested in the health of our democracy must accept that improving the quality of news will ultimately require a number of different, pragmatic, and interrelated approaches. Most news reporters see their jobs as providing the public with the most accurate, timely, and useful information necessary to effectively engage in civic life. The role of the nonprofit community should be to help provide journalists with the means to do so. Regulatory approaches designed to develop and enforce public interest obligations can help provide this. So too can efforts to strengthen public broadcasting. But given the political and economic realities within which the commercial news media operate, we should complement these approaches with efforts intended to demonstrate that what is good for democracy can in fact be good for the media industry.

## Notes

1. Gilliam, F. D., and Iyengar, S. "Prime Suspects: The Influence of Local Television News on the Viewing Public." *American Journal of Political Science,* 2000, p. 560.

2. The analog spectrum consists of relatively slow modulating radio waves. Broadcasters use various frequencies of radio waves on the analog spectrum to transmit both sounds and images through the air.

3. The digital spectrum consists of relatively fast modulating waves that are ideal for carrying computer-generated digital information through the air. Digital broadcasting requires a computer to send and receive information whereas analog broadcasting does not.

4. The national media also did a poor job covering debates, airing only one of the eight Republican presidential primaries in the 2000 election (with the others superseded by entertainment programming such as the World Wrestling Federation's "Smackdown").

5. The Torricelli Amendment would have decreased the amount that local stations could charge candidates for TV commercials, theoretically making it more affordable to mount a campaign. The amendment was defeated in the House version of the bill as the result of an intense lobbying effort by broadcasters.

6. One version of the free airtime idea backed by the Alliance for Better Campaigns would require local broadcasters to provide in the thirty days before election day at least five minutes of free airtime a night, during prime viewing hours, to local candidates to express their views.

7. Traditionally the news operation has been viewed as a source of pride to local broadcasters and not a source of revenue.

*Sean P. Treglia is a program officer in the Public Policy program of The Pew Charitable Trusts.*

# Fixing Elections: The Failure of America's Winner-Take-All Politics

*Steven Hill*

> It has been said that democracy is the worst form of government—
> except all those other forms that have been tried from time to time.
>
> —Winston Churchill

Voter turnout levels in the single digits are becoming more common across the country. The numbers would be comical if they weren't so dismaying: in recent mayoral elections turnout ranged from 5 percent in Dallas to 6 percent in Charlotte, 7 percent in Austin, and 7.5 percent in San Antonio.[1] Other equally dismal showings include a 6 percent turnout for a gubernatorial primary in Kentucky[2] and 3 percent for a statewide runoff in North Carolina.[3] Several cities and towns in southeastern Massachusetts have reported single-digit turnouts,[4] and the 2000 state primary election in Massachusetts drew less than 10 percent, a modern record low according to the Massachusetts Secretary of State.[5] In the 1997 primary for attorney general of Virginia, the commonwealth's top law enforcement official, a whopping 5 percent of registered voters turned out, the lowest figure since 1949.[6]

In seven cities in Los Angeles County, elections for city council were *canceled* when no challengers emerged to oppose the safe-seat incumbents.[7] When less than half of the eligible voters bothered to vote in the 1996 presidential election, it was the lowest turnout in the last seventy years; the 2000 election was barely an improvement.[8] For all the pyrotechnics generated by the 2000 presidential unelection, it is easy to forget that nearly half of the eligible voters once again sat it out. More people watched the Super Bowl or the TV fad *Survivor* than cast ballots for either Gore or Bush.[9]

*Note:* This article has been adapted with permission of the publisher from *Fixing Elections: The Failure of America's Winner-Take-All Politics,* by Steven Hill, Routledge, 2002.

Turnout for the 1998 congressional elections dipped even further, to just under a third of eligible voters, despite the first midterm use of motor voter laws, which greatly boosted voter registration rolls. The 2000 congressional elections managed a marginally higher showing.[10] However, a week of *Who Wants to Be a Millionaire?* and O.J.'s freeway ride in his white Bronco drew comparable numbers.[11] Voter turnout in the world's lone remaining superpower has fallen to 138th in the world—sandwiched between Botswana and Chad.[12] Perhaps most disturbing, only 12 percent of eighteen- to twenty-four-year-olds and 8.5 percent of eighteen- to nineteen-year-olds voted in the 1998 congressional elections.[13] The future adults of America have tuned out and dropped out, electorally speaking, even more than their 1960s hippie forebears.[14]

Rational choice theorists have long looked askance at the individual act of voting, and evidently to more and more Americans, voting seems increasingly pointless and a waste of precious time.[15] The voting incentive in recent years has seriously eroded, producing what Anthony Downs once called a "rationality crisis."[16] The increasingly fractious political divisions in the country, epitomized by both Clinton's impeachment and the outcome of the 2000 election, compound the significance of this persistent pattern of low voter turnout.

How deep these divisions go is the subject of continuing debate. The red-and-blue map used to indicated the states won by Bush or Gore shows stark regional differences in the appeal of the two national parties. These partisan differences are interlaced with economic and social divisions. Furthermore, events such as the statewide referendum in Mississippi in April 2001 that retained the use of Confederate symbols on the state flag[17] demonstrate the still-potent racial polarization in the country. The police shooting last year in Cincinnati of an unarmed black man, which resulted in four days of the worst street fighting since the death of Martin Luther King Jr., graphically illustrates the volatility of racial relations in the nation's cities. Given these and other strains in our political system, the disengagement of citizens, as reflected in the low voting rate, is a matter of serious concern.

A multitude of assessments, observations, and claims can be adduced to diagnose the present situation, evaluate its significance, and provide counsel as to what needs to be done. My concern here is to highlight the deficiencies of the *winner-take-all* voting system as it affects the healthy functioning of our democracy. A voting system comprises the rules and practices that determine how votes are translated into who wins elections. It has a considerable, if often overlooked, impact on the defining characteristics of a democratic republic: representation, participation, political discourse and campaigns, legislative policy, and national unity.

## Winner-Take-All's Dubious Democracy

The U.S. political system is a work in progress, and throughout our history there has been a recurrent need to find ways of adapting the original eighteenth-century structures and institutions to changing circumstances. Winner-take-all elections are at the heart of what is essentially a two-party political system that distorts representation, limits participation, and exerts a host of ill-considered effects on the ways campaigns are run and legislative policy is made. Amid dramatically shifting racial, regional, and partisan demographics, modern campaign techniques like polling, focus groups, and thirty-second TV sound bites challenge the ability of our geographic-based, two-party system to promote democratic governance. Nowhere is this more apparent than in the basic relationship of representation.

**Representation.** By design, a winner-take-all voting system represents majority constituencies to the detriment of minority constituencies. Minority in this context applies simply to the voters in the electoral district whose candidate did not win. While this might often refer to racial minorities, in many districts minority status denotes so-called orphaned Democratic or Republican voters who live in districts dominated by the opposing party. In such cases, the logic of winner-take-all representation posits that the elected official will adequately represent the interests of residents of the geographical area despite differences in party affiliation. This complacent assumption appears increasingly dubious against the backdrop of declining party affiliation and increasing diversity.

Representation has become balkanized with many cities being Democratic Party strongholds while a number of rural and suburban areas, especially in the West and the South, are dominated by Republicans. This concentration of political strength has led to the emergence of political monocultures, created by an overrepresentation of the majority party. The political impact of this concentration is augmented by the disproportionate influence that low-population states have in the U.S. Senate and the Electoral College. At present, this representation "subsidy," based on the equal number of senators in each state regardless of population, disproportionately favors conservative representation, policy, and issues. According to political scientists Francis E. Lee and Bruce I. Oppenheimer, in their book *Sizing Up the Senate: The Unequal Consequences of Equal Representation,* this representation quota has over-represented the Republican Party in the Senate in every election since 1958, primarily due to Republican success in low-population, conservative states in the West and South. Given the way we elect presidents, the small state advantage can play a role in skewing the outcome in the Electoral College such that the winner of the popular vote can lose the election.

**Participation.** Despite the pyrotechnics at the photo finish of the 2000 presidential contest, most elections have been turned into pale farces of competition, and by extension, of participation. Voter turnout for our national legislature regularly drops well below a majority, often barely a third, of the adult population. Nine out of ten U.S. House races regularly are won by noncompetitive margins of at least 10 percentage points, and three-quarters by landslide margins of at least 20 percentage points. Furthermore, the 2002 redistricting plans in most states amounted to little better than incumbent protection plans, producing even fewer competitive districts than previous redistricting had. State legislative elections are even worse; in recent years an average of two out of five state legislative races were uncontested by one of the two major parties. The partisan demographics in these districts are so lopsided that the disadvantaged party considers it a waste of resources to run a candidate. Voters thus have little choice but to ratify the candidate or abstain from voting. The frame of reference for these voters is no longer a two-party system, it is a *one*-party system.

Redistricting is the twin sibling of the winner-take-all system—you don't get one without the other. Instead of voters choosing the politicians, the politicians are choosing the voters via the redistricting process, which is increasingly dominated by technocrats using the precision of sophisticated computers and demographic data.

Even campaign finance reform will provide little relief, given the political terrain of lopsided partisan demographics and regional polarization capped by gerrymandered districts. Millions of citizens in noncompetitive districts and states have few viable choices when they step into the voting booth. Instead, voters have lots of opportunities to waste their votes on losers and third party spoilers or to hold their noses and vote for the "lesser of two evils." Not surprisingly, voters have quit responding to the uninspiring electoral choices regularly manufactured by the winner-take-all system.

**Political Discourse and Campaigns.**   The technologies and tactics used in commercial marketing, such as polling, focus groups, and thirty-second TV spots, are well suited to the two-choice, two-candidate milieu of winner-take-all politics. With the ideological space relatively wide open and undefined in a two-choice field, candidates and their consultants are free to game the system by reducing complex policy proposals into campaign slogans and sound bites, carving out positions vis-à-vis their lone opponent. Without any third candidate intervening with conflicting messages, the parties have little need to watch their backs; when partisan supporters have no other electoral place to go they can be taken for granted, freeing candidates to target undecided swing voters. The use of modern campaign techniques is producing McCampaigns of centrist rhetoric and images designed to appeal to these voters.

The way candidates and parties now conduct their campaigns means real political exchange and discourse gets buried, and we lose political ideas. Voters are not challenged or stimulated to think about the great issues of our times, because these issues mostly are left on the political sidelines. The two-party bias of our winner-take-all voting system does not allow the flowering of new parties or independent candidacies that can act as laboratories for new ideas or give voters other viable choices. Tragically, at a time of rapid technological, ecological, and global change, when fresh, creative ideas for dealing with looming challenges and crises are at a premium, our nation is in the throes of an alarming loss of political ideas.

*Legislative Policy.* The effects of the winner-take-all voting system on campaigns, voter participation, and representation affect the composition of legislative bodies and the formulation of policy at both the national and the state levels. Unlike a proportional representation system, where political parties get legislative seats in proportion to the votes they win, the winner-take-all system means one party can receive less than 50 percent of the national vote yet take more than 50 percent of the seats. Between 1945 and 1980, this has happened in the House of Representatives 17 percent of the time. In the 2000 elections for the U.S. House, there were 371 seats for which both Democrats and Republicans fielded a candidate, and even though the Democrats won slightly more votes nationwide in those races, the Republicans won more of the seats, by a margin of 191 to 179 (plus one independent) due to the vagaries of how the district lines were drawn.

In the U.S. Senate the representation subsidy given to low-population states has had dramatic influences on policy, particularly federal subsidies to states. As Lee and Oppenheimer have pointed out in *Sizing Up the Senate,* the overrepresentation of the least populous states means the Senate has a tendency to design policies that distribute federal dollars disproportionately to those states, with the result that these states receive more federal funds per capita than the most populous states. This overrepresentation affects other policy areas as well. Over the years, conservative senators from low-population states, representing a small fragment of the nation's population, have been instrumental in slowing down or thwarting policy initiatives dealing with New Deal programs, desegregation, affirmative action, campaign finance reform, health care reform, gun control, and more.

*National Unity.* Before the upsurge in domestic unity following the September 11 attacks, numerous pundits and commentators had observed that the general level of national division and partisan warfare had reached unsettling proportions. Even with the unifying stimulus of foreign aggression, by December 28, 2001, *USA Today* was running headlines like "Lawmakers Back at Each Other's Throats." Given how the winner-take-all nature of our electoral contests exacerbates the stakes, and hence the division and conflict, this decline of comity is hardly surprising.

Regional balkanization and the centrist tilt to campaigns in search of undecided voters make it difficult for either national political party to act as a vehicle to address, much less resolve, genuine conflicts over social issues. According to some estimates, as many as forty-one states, representing 436 of the 538 Electoral College votes, are considered safe or mostly leaning to one party or the other. That leaves only nine states, and 102 electoral votes, as the campaign battleground in the 2004 election. With the two parties effectively acting as proxies for differing regional, cultural, and racial interests, the opportunities for cooperation and cross-fertilization of ideas are scarce.

## The Fork in the Road

The winner-take-all voting system is depriving voters of viable choices and is contributing to the decline in voter participation and engagement. This voting system distorts representation by orphaning millions of Democratic and Republican voters who live in jurisdictions dominated by rival party supporters, to say nothing of its effects on supporters of third party candidates. The tendency to regional polarization is exacerbating national tensions while producing an alarming debasement of campaigns and political discourse. The dynamics unleashed by winner-take-all voting affect how much money is needed to run a viable campaign, how the media cover those campaigns, and how political ideas are debated and decided. Finally, the voting system is draining the vitality out of well-meaning political reforms like campaign finance reform. In short, winner-take-all is making *losers* of us all.

Even the apparent winners lose when our representative democracy is so sickly. As most players (voters) abandon the field in frustration, the game is left to be played by increasingly partisan careerists and professionals and by the most zealous activists who seize center stage, further polarizing politics and policy. And as politics become more polarized, negative, and downright nasty, more and more people turn off and tune out.

We should all be concerned about the political destiny of our nation, characterized as the present is by decreasing voter turnout and diminishing electoral engagement yet also rife with acrimony and political division along the volatile lines of partisanship, regionalism, and racial and cultural polarization.

The developing trend of regional balkanization—exacerbated by our winner-take-all practices—is alarmingly suggestive of the geographic-based polarization faced by other large winner-take-all democracies such as India and Canada. The gravity of the moment requires a new term to describe what may be emerging: *post-democracy.* By that I mean a polarized, splintered nation that is nominally democratic yet has fewer and fewer voters. A nation where the civil institutions are still vital and individual rights are reasonably well protected, but where campaigns fail to catalyze public deliberation and elections fail to mobilize political energies.

Post-democracy is a type of polity in which huge numbers of citizens simply have given up because they don't think politics or elections matter in their lives. They have made a decision, conscious or otherwise, that political and electoral participation is a waste of time and that withdrawing makes more sense, despite its obvious perils. Even though post-democracy is a political iceberg of staggering proportions, there is every reason to believe that reform of our voting system can open new avenues for participation and engagement. Ending the winner-take-all system could make politics more meaningful for more people and lead to a better democracy rather than a post-democracy. More than a century later, government of, by, and for the people remains a revolutionary and fragile concept.

## Notes

1. Voter turnout numbers for Dallas, San Antonio, Austin, and Charlotte taken from the Web site of the Dallas County Elections, 1999 mayoral election results, [www.dalcoelections.org/election99/index.html]; the Web site of the City of Austin, [www.ci.austin.tx.us/election] (though it appears both Dallas and Austin list registered voter turnout instead of eligible voter turnout, making their actual turnouts lower than their listed figures); Berke, R. "Incumbent Big City Mayors Are Sitting Pretty." *New York Times,* Nov. 2, 1997; and Flores, H. "Are Single-Member Districts More Competitive Than At-Large Elections?" Paper presented at the annual meeting of the American Political Science Association, 1999.

2. Crowley, P. "Voters May Be Scarce in N. Ky." *Cincinnati Enquirer,* Oct. 31, 1999.

3. Kleppner, C. "N.C. Could Avoid Costly Runoff Elections." *Raleigh News and Observer,* May 10, 2000.

4. "Rain, rain go away, come again another day." *Standard-Times,* Sept. 18, 1996. [www.s-t.com/daily/09-96/09-18-96/b07lo092.htm].

5. "Politicians Got What They Wanted Tuesday" (Editorial). *Lawrence (Mass.) Eagle-Tribune,* Sept. 22, 2000.

6. Virginia State Board of Elections. [www.sbe.state.va.us].

7. Shuit, D. P. "Lack of Interest Cancels Some Local Elections." *Los Angeles Times,* Feb. 21, 1999.

8. Heilprin, J. "105.4 Million Voters Cast Ballots," Dec. 18, 2000. [www.ap.org]. Voter turnout for the 2000 presidential election was 105,380,929 ballots cast, or 50.7 percent of those eligible, according to Curtis B. Gans, director of the Committee for the Study of the American Electorate. That figure was up slightly from 49 percent in 1996 but significantly lower than the 62.8 percent who voted in 1960, making the 2000 election among those with the lowest turnouts. Interestingly, among sixteen battleground states where the race was hotly contested, turnout increased by an average of 3.4 percent, compared with a 1.6 percent increase in other states. In ten states where the race wasn't close—Arizona, Hawaii, Idaho, Kansas, Louisiana, Montana, New Jersey, Oklahoma, South Dakota, and Wyoming—the turnout was lower than in 1996. See Federal Elections Commission. "Voter Registration and Turnout—1996." [www.fec.gov/pages/96to.htm].

9. Fifty-one million viewers watched the season finale of *Survivor,* according to *Newsweek* ("Reality TV's Real Survivor," Dec. 25, 2000, p. 77). The 2000 Super Bowl was watched by over forty-three million households, according to *USA Today* ("Why the NFL Rules" [Editorial], Dec. 22, 2000), which translates into roughly 120 to 130 million viewers. Al Gore, the winner of the 2000 presidential popular vote, had 50.9 million votes, which was the most votes for any presidential candidate since Ronald Reagan.

10. The average voter turnout in House midterm elections from 1982 to 1994 was 37 percent, and in presidential election years the House turnout was 48 percent—in both instances less than a majority of eligible voters (*Statistical Abstract of the United States.* Washington, D.C.: Government Printing Office, 1998, p. 297). The turnout has been declining in the past decade, with fewer than 33 percent of eligible voters turning out for the 1998 midterm congressional elections. In that year motor voter laws boosted registration roles by 5.5 million to include 64 percent of eligible voters, the highest since 1970. Yet voter turnout still declined to its lowest level since 1942, as 115 million Americans who were eligible to vote chose not to do so, according to the Center for Voting and Democracy. "Dubious Democracy 2000." [www.fairvote.org/2001/usa.htm]. Also see "1998 Turnout Hits 36 Percent, Lowest Since World War II." *The Political Standard* (Alliance for Better Campaigns newsletter). [www.bettercampaigns.org].

11. According to Johnston, D. C. ("Voting, America's Not Keen On. Coffee Is Another Matter." *New York Times,* Nov. 10, 1996, p. E2), an estimated 95 million people watched O.J. Simpson take his freeway ride, and 92.8 million cast ballots in the 1996 general elections.

12. See "Voter Turnout for 1945 to 1997: A Global Report on Political Participation." Institute for Democracy and Electoral Assistance, 1997. [www.idea.int].

13. Youth voter turnout figures are from Curtis Gans of the Committee for the Study of the American Electorate. Voter turnout of eighteen- to nineteen-year-olds in the 1994 midterm elections was 14.5 percent, which means voter turnout among this demographic group dropped an astounding 41 percent between 1994 and 1998. Voter News Service estimated that 38.6 percent of eighteen- to twenty-nine-year-olds made it to the polls in the 2000 election. See Sandoz, W. "GenY Voter Turnout Increased, Experts Say." *Medill News Service,* Nov. 8, 2000. Typically, youth voter turnout drops by about 50 percent from presidential election year to nonpresidential (midterm) election year. According to a National Association of Secretaries of State study, youth electoral participation reveals a portrait of an increasingly disconnected and apathetic generation. Since the 1972 presidential election, when the voting age was lowered to eighteen, there has been almost a 20 percent decrease in voting among eighteen- to twenty-four-year-olds, with only 32 percent going to the polls in 1996, a presidential election year. See "State Secretaries Push Major Youth Voting Initiative, New Millennium Project: Why Young People Don't Vote." [www.nass.org].

14. One recent survey by UCLA's Higher Education Research Institute found a record low interest in politics among new college freshmen in 2000, with 28.1 percent of respondents inclined to keep up with political affairs and 16.4 percent saying they discuss politics frequently. Although that was only a slight decline from last year, nevertheless it was significant because "freshmen interest in politics traditionally increases during a presidential election year," rather than decreases, said survey director Linda Sax. Historically, these results on political-engagement questions show a long, steady decline, with highs in these two categories at 60.3 percent and 33.6 percent, reached in the late 1960s. See M. B. Marklein, "Female Freshmen Doubt Tech Skills, College Survey Also Shows Record-Low Interest in Politics." *USA Today,* Jan. 22, 2001. A 1999 Field poll found that in 1983, 35 percent of young adults between the ages of eighteen and twenty-nine said they followed civic events most of the time, but only 23 percent said they did so in 1999. That decline was exhibited also among individuals ages thirty to thirty-nine, where interest in government and politics dropped from 44 percent to 27 percent in the same period. See "Californians (Ho-Hum) Cool to Politics (Yawn)." *San Francisco Examiner,* Apr. 30, 1999, p. A7.

15. By way of contrast, in certain European nations a less-than-majority turnout for national referendums automatically voids the election. Using that standard, virtually all U.S. elections would be nullified.

16. Downs, A. *Economic Theory of Democracy.* New York: HarperCollins, 1957, p. 139.

17. Over two-thirds of Mississippi voters chose to retain the Confederate symbols on their state flag, in a racially split vote. The civil rights era still haunts Southern memories. "As Mississippians voted to keep the Confederate cross on their flag, jury selection was under way in Alabama for the trial of a white man accused in the 1963 bombing of Birmingham's Sixteenth Street Baptist Church, which killed four black girls. Several civil-rights cases have recently been reopened, including some in Mississippi. But the Confederate flag remains the main lightning rod of controversy. Last year, the National Association for the Advancement of Colored People led an economic boycott of South Carolina, bringing the eventual removal of a Confederate flag from the statehouse dome. Three months ago, Georgia's legislators opted to shrink a Confederate symbol that had dominated that state's flag since 1956. Throughout Alabama, cities and counties have stopped flying the state's flag, which bears a strong resemblance to the Confederate banner. In most of these cases, pressure from white business to change was as great as that from black politicians. Indeed, Mississippi's vote can also be seen as a rearguard action in the battle between rural white traditionalists and the proponents of a New South" ("Not as simple as it looks." *The Economist,* Apr. 19, 2001).

*Steven Hill is western regional director for the Center for Voting and Democracy. More information on reforming the U.S. election system can be found on the center's Web site, www.fairvote.org.*

# Big Wins for Democracy: San Francisco and Vermont Vote for Instant Runoff Voting

*Eric C. Olson, Steven Hill*

The electoral reform option of *instant runoff voting* (IRV) is continuing to win approval at the ballot box. In March 2002, San Francisco voters supported IRV for citywide elections by an impressive 55 to 45 percent margin, while citizens at over fifty town meetings across Vermont overwhelmingly voted to urge state lawmakers to adopt IRV for statewide elections. Fifty-two out of fifty-four Vermont towns considering the IRV advisory question supported the reform. In Burlington, the state's largest city, the question appeared as a ballot measure rather than at a traditional town meeting. Burlington voters approved the measure by better than a two-to-one margin.

IRV allows voters to rank candidates in the order of their preference—1, 2, 3, and so on. If none of the candidates wins a clear majority, second-ranked (that is, *runoff*) votes are used to decide the winner. The candidate with the lowest vote total is eliminated and the second-choice votes on those ballots are added to the first-choice totals for the other candidates. If necessary, the process is repeated until a winner emerges by majority vote. Thus, not only does IRV ensure that majority winners are decided in one election but the impact of "spoiler" candidates and wasted votes is minimized. IRV allows voters to express their true preferences without increasing the chance of throwing the election to the candidate they like the least.

The big story in both breakthrough victories was the power of citizen activists and organizational coalitions that made the difference.

## San Francisco

In San Francisco, despite well-funded opposition from the city's downtown business establishment, a determined citizen brigade staffed the phones and took to the streets, knocking on doors, leafleting, and generating visibility for the Yes on Prop A campaign over the last two months before the vote. Staff from the San Francisco office of the Center for Voting and Democracy (CVD) organized the campaign, and local volunteers came from California PIRG, the Green Party, Californians for Proportional Representation, and assorted activist circles. Efforts by organizational friends, including Common Cause, also contributed heavily to the outcome. The support of important political leaders, including the president of the Board of Supervisors, Tom Ammiano, and California Assembly Majority Leader Kevin Shelley (who on election day won a Democratic primary for secretary of state), was also one of the key components in the measure's success.

CVD's longstanding advocacy of alternative voting systems helped to prime the electorate on the issue, and its outreach to other organizations helped create a successful coalition. Local CVD staff have attracted newspaper attention to the cause over the years, pointing out the problems of traditional, "delayed" runoff elections as well as the shortcomings of plurality voting and other electoral problems. Staff from the San Francisco office managed the 1996 campaign for proportional representation and organized, with Common Cause, the successful ballot measure for public financing of elections in 2000. As part of the Yes on Prop A campaign, CVD staff won endorsements from Common Cause, the Sierra Club, Chinese for Affirmative Action, the local NOW Chapter, the League of Conservation Voters, the city's Democratic Party, the AFL-CIO Labor Council, and Democratic Clubs such as the Harvey Milk LGBT Democratic Club, the Latino Democratic Club, and the Asian Pacific Democratic Club. Tenant groups, individual labor unions, and seniors organizations also endorsed Proposition A. In addition, when the city was looking at purchasing new voting machines, CVD staff worked with the city's election administrators to ensure that new voting equipment could handle ranked ballots.

In the final weeks of the campaign, the downtown business–funded opposition (rumored to have spent upwards of $100,000) unleashed several misleading "hit" pieces. All along the opponents had lobbed misinformation at voters, claiming that under instant runoffs "a computer chip," not voters, would decide elections. In the last week, however, using the benign-sounding moniker of San Franciscans for Voter Rights, they got deep into the mud by distributing literature in Chinatown featuring Chinese tanks at Tiananmen Square and maintaining that IRV would take away democracy. They also targeted women voters with a scare piece comparing IRV supporters to antisuffragists. In the end, both major newspapers opposed Prop A, although both newspapers had run commentaries and articles that were previously sympathetic toward the reform's goals.

Despite all this opposition, on election day Prop A prevailed, reminding onlookers of Victor Hugo's famous observation, "There's no greater army than an idea whose time has come."

## Vermont

Former Progressive Party state legislator and CVD staffer Terry Bouricius has been working on IRV in Vermont since 1998, when he was able to get the legislature to appoint a committee of professors, good government groups, and others to explore the issue. They produced a favorable report, and he has worked newspapers and elected officials ever since to pursue the reform. Along the way, Bouricius has cultivated constructive relationships with grassroots organizations and gained endorsements from a variety of groups ranging from Common Cause to the conservative, agriculture-based organization the Grange. Bouricius worked in part through the state's League of Women Voters chapter, which wholeheartedly believes in IRV and was instrumental in placing IRV on the town meeting agendas throughout the state.

Over the course of the last couple of years, many of the Green Mountain State's top elected officials have come to support IRV, including Governor Howard Dean (D), Secretary of State Deb Markowitz (D), and Congressperson Bernie Sanders (I). Dean's challengers in the 2000 election, Republican Ruth Dwyer, and Progressive Party candidate Anthony Pollina both supported IRV—Dwyer had cosponsored instant runoff legislation in the legislature.

Unlike San Francisco, Vermont had no organized opposition to IRV (although a number of Republicans expressed their dislike for it). But the real opposition in any campaign like this is always ignorance, because voters will vote no unless they are comfortable with a measure, even if the measure is only advisory. Bouricius, the League of Women Voters, and other supporters of the Vermont effort overcame this hurdle through sustained education, keeping the issue in the newspapers, highlighting the issue on talk radio, and identifying strong, respected speakers for nearly every town meeting.

## A Look Ahead

The San Francisco and Vermont wins have attracted national attention, and as the unfamiliarity hurdle is lowered the prospects for other efforts should continue to improve. At present, the work to expand IRV in the Bay Area and throughout California is continuing, and in Vermont it's time to capitalize and push for a win in the state legislature to implement the reform. Activists have made progress in legislatures in Washington state and New Mexico in recent years, and Alaska will hold a referendum on August 27, 2002. While cities are great places to focus efforts at reform, so too are schools, nonprofit organizations, and other organizations that hold elections. The ideal city profile seems to be a liberal to progressive city where a significant cost savings will be realized by eliminating a runoff or primary election when voter turnout is typically half that of the November election. Such a confluence of characteristics allows reformers to attract good government types and liberal supporters of reform, as well as fiscal conservatives.

Although local wins hold promise of extending IRV to the election of partisan state and federal officeholders, high-profile national demonstrations of the problems inherent in the existing electoral system, most notably the 2000 presidential election, can also increase the appeal of the reform. IRV allows people to feel freer to vote for third party candidates instead of being deterred by the lesser-of-two-evils argument. This outcome would send a clearer policy direction to the ultimate winner because it would more accurately reflect the true sympathies of the electorate.

Through sustained efforts, a persistent critique of the existing election system, and close ties to community organizations and good government groups, pro democracy advocates won big on March 5 in San Francisco. The future of such crucial reform relies on building from these wins and cultivating more of these relationships across the nation. IRV provides a fix to some of the key challenges facing electoral politics; activists need to keep the momentum going. To learn more, visit the San Francisco campaign Web site, www.improvetherunoff.com, or the Center for Voting and Democracy Web site: www.fairvote.org.

*Eric C. Olson is deputy director of the Center for Voting and Democracy.*

*Steven Hill is western regional director for the Center for Voting and Democracy, author of* Fixing Elections: The Failure of America's Winner-Take-All Politics, *and was campaign manager for Proposition A.*

# States and Campaign Finance Reform

*David Schultz*

The role of money in politics at the state level is increasingly coming to resemble the familiar dynamics long entrenched in federal campaigns and elections. A general pattern of increased costs associated with running for election includes growth in average and aggregate contributions and expenditures and a rise in the use of issue advocacy, soft money, and independent expenditures by both party and nonparty organizations and individuals. These developments have fueled concerns about the influence of special interests on elections and policymaking and incumbency advantages that limit the competitiveness of elections. However, states have considerable latitude to experiment with novel approaches for dealing with these concerns.

## The Changing Realities of State Campaigns

*Increased Campaign Costs.* States of all sizes are experiencing dramatic increases in campaign costs, making it more difficult for individuals to challenge incumbents and wealthy candidates. For example, in 1976, the total aggregate spending for state-level races in California was $20 million, while in 2000 it was $130 million. In Iowa, total contributions to state legislative campaigns increased from $3,606,739 in 1994 to $9,800,515 in 2000. Finally, in the 2000 Oklahoma elections, Senate legislative candidates on average raised $53,572, while House candidates raised $27,647; both represented significant increases from previous election cycles.

*Soft Money.* Soft money is also becoming a problem, particularly in Minnesota, Florida, South Carolina, Indiana, and California. In Minnesota over the last several years, soft money totals have far exceeded those for hard money. In 1994, soft money totaled $5.9 million while in 2000 it was $20 million. This compares to total hard money in those years of $3.1 and $7.8 million, respectively. Moreover, Minnesota, Iowa, South Carolina, and Florida (especially after the 2000 ballot disputes) have seen large influxes of national party and other out-of-state money into state parties. In Minnesota, both the Democratic and the Republican state political parties received well over $1.5 million dollars from their respective national parties to fuel get out the vote campaigns, issue ads, and other activities.

Efforts to regulate soft money have met with mixed results. In 1996, Alaska enacted a total ban on soft money contributions that was later declared unconstitutional by a federal district court. That decision is still under appeal. In contrast, since 1999, Connecticut has banned soft money transfers from national to state political parties. As a result, soft money transfers into the state have decreased with no apparent efforts to evade compliance with the law.

**Independent Expenditures.** Many states, including Texas, Minnesota, Oklahoma, and California, have recorded a rise in independent expenditures and the use of issue ads by parties and PACs. (Although a similar increase has not occurred in Indiana and Illinois, the absence of limits on individual contributions in those states likely limits interest in these types of efforts.) There has also been an increase in party independent expenditures since the 1996 *Colorado Republican Party v. Federal Election Commission* Supreme Court decision declared bans on them to be unconstitutional. In Minnesota, since the state law making party independent expenditures illegal was struck down as unconstitutional, this type of spending increased by 439 percent from 1998 to 2000.

Regulation of independent expenditures is difficult. The courts have ruled that it is unconstitutional to ban or limit them because they constitute a form of free speech. Mandatory disclosure of independent expenditures at the time they are made, such as in Minnesota and Maine, seems to be the only direct regulation the courts will permit. However, the First Circuit Federal Court of Appeals has upheld Maine's system of voluntary public financing to offset the impact of independent expenditures on candidates who participate in their public financing system. At present it is unclear how successful that law will be.

**Lobbyist Activity.** A fourth, and often overlooked, area where money affects politics is lobbying. Special interests will often hire lobbyists to advance their political interests instead of, or in addition to, giving money to candidates and political parties. Groups often spend more money on lobbying than any other activity.

Lobbyist activity has grown significantly at the state level over the last few years. In Oklahoma, a state where lobbyists are required to register and disclose many of their financial activities, the number of lobbyists for PACs has grown steadily from 83 in 1976 to 466 in 2000. In Florida, lobbying has become a game of intense specialization. In a phenomenon dubbed "team lobbying," groups of as many as fifty lobbyists will pursue a coordinated strategy to advocate major legislation. Republicans lobby Republican legislators, Democrats lobby Democratic legislators, African Americans lobby African American legislators, and women lobby female legislators. In Minnesota, PACs and lobbyists spent over $15 million in 2000 to influence state elections and public policy, of which $5.4 million was spent on lobbying. This was more than was given by PACs or other groups in hard or soft money donations.

Lobbyist disbursements beyond the salary of lobbyists often include money spent on gifts to state legislators, including free travel, meals, and other benefits. These gifts create a cozy atmosphere between legislators and lobbyists, thereby giving the latter more influence or access to the former.

Many states have tried to regulate lobbyist activity. Oklahoma, Wisconsin, Minnesota, Florida, and South Carolina require those who meet the statutory definition of a lobbyist to register with the state, and they are also required to disclose many of their financial dealings and activities. Minnesota and Wisconsin ban lobbyists from giving publicbofficials any gifts, including meals and refreshments, while South Carolina limits the type and value of gifts that can be given. North and South Carolina as well as Minnesota prevent lobbyists from making political donations to state legislators while they are in session. Finally, Minnesota and Maine limit how much money lobbyists can donate to candidates as a condition of the latter receiving public funding for their campaigns.

All of these options help to lessen lobbyist influence, but ultimately the Constitution prevents an outright ban on lobbyist activity.

**Summary.** A familiar adage claims that regulating money in politics is like squeezing a water balloon: pressure at one end merely pushes the water elsewhere. Regulations that seek to limit money in politics do not seem to prevent contributors from giving; they simply shift their donations to another venue. The preceding discussion focused on four general areas of political spending: hard money contributions to candidates, soft money contributions to parties and political groups, independent expenditures, and lobbying. The record of activity at the state level indicates that individuals and interest groups shift their resources among these options depending upon the prevailing regulatory structure and their organizational tactics and goals.

## Lessons from State Campaign Finance Reform Efforts

Although exploring campaign financing in all fifty states is beyond the scope of this article, some conclusions and recommendations can be made.

**Disclosure Alone Is Not Enough.** There is little evidence that disclosure alone is enough to address the problems associated with money and politics. Disclosure laws vary from state to state, and it can be difficult to judge their effect. Some states require disclosure of all donations down to a certain threshold, with that threshold varying from $50 to $500 or more. Some states do not require some parties to disclose, some do not make disclosure mandatory, and some set dates for filing that are so late that no citizen could ever review the information in time to make an electoral choice. Additionally, some states, such as Texas, have no real enforcement power to mandate disclosure. And in states where electronic disclosure is used (an innovation that "disclosure only" advocates trumpet) the disclosure is often not mandatory or is spotty at best.

Although some evidence indicates that the competitiveness of races in Iowa and Indiana may be partially due to the lack of limits on contributions, state experience in general indicates that disclosure alone does not produce more competitive races or equalize the spending inequities between challengers and incumbents. Several state studies note the overwhelming power of incumbents to raise money compared to challengers.

*The Need for Public Funding.* A review of state regulatory mechanisms mandating disclosure or various combinations of disclosure and contribution limits indicates that the only state demonstrating any evidence of remedying incumbent advantage is Minnesota. As discussed below, the partial public financing system established in Minnesota has much to do with that. Term limits may be thought of as an extreme cure for the problems posed by incumbent advantage. But as studies of Michigan reveal, term limits by themselves do not produce more competitive races. Instead they have generated more reliance on a candidate's own money to run for office as well as an increased role for party and PAC giving. There is no evidence that term limits have severed the connection between legislators and special interests or have produced a more diversified legislature; instead, such limits seem to be generating wealthier candidates. Thus, for those seeking to mitigate the power of incumbency and produce more competitive elections, neither disclosure alone nor term limits seem to be the solution. Instead, some move toward public funding is needed.

## Two Examples of Public Funding

Two of the more innovative efforts to address the growing impact of money on state elections and policymaking can be found in Minnesota and in Maine, Massachusetts, and Arizona. Minnesota has adopted a partial public financing system while Maine, Massachusetts, and Arizona have opted for total public funding.

*Minnesota.* Minnesota has an extensive system of partial public financing for state legislative and constitutional offices. There are limits on how much a candidate can spend to run for an office and how much can be taken from PACS, lobbyists, and big donors. Candidates who agree to the spending limits receive a subsidy from the state that is equal to half of the spending limit for that office. Spending limits are also adjusted in certain cases such as for first-time challengers or when an opponent does not participate in the public subsidy program. Money to finance this system comes from income tax checkoffs and an appropriation from the state general fund.

Candidates also can receive additional public money from a unique rebate program whereby each adult can donate up to $50 per year to a participating candidate or candidates and have that money rebated to them from the state. Between the rebate and public subsidy programs, candidates for office in Minnesota can effectively receive most of the money they need to run for office. Minnesota has had this system for years, with nearly 100 percent participation in both programs. The impact of the law has been to significantly equalize spending between challengers and incumbents, thereby producing more competitive elections. It even allowed for the election of third party gubernatorial candidate Jesse Ventura in 1998.

Minnesota has enacted other laws to address the role of money in state politics. There are significant disclosure laws for candidates, parties, PACs, and lobbyists. Lobbyists may not give any gifts of any value—even a cup of coffee—to any elected or other state official. In 1991, the state tried to address the problem of independent expenditures by providing an additional public subsidy to a participating candidate who was the target of such expenditure or whose opponent benefited from one. However, the Eighth Circuit Court of Appeals declared the law unconstitutional. Minnesota has not addressed the issue of soft money, which is becoming a growing problem in the state.

**Maine, Massachusetts, and Arizona.**  Maine, Massachusetts, and Arizona have passed what is called the "Clean Money" or total public financing option. Clean Money is a movement that gained momentum in the mid-1990s. In the fall of 1995 more than 1,200 clean election volunteers in Maine collected 65,000 signatures to put the "Maine Clean Elections Act" on the 1996 ballot. That measure passed and took effect for the 2000 elections. About one-third of the candidates for state office opted to participate in the total public financing system. So far only Maine has any experience with the Clean Money option. Similar laws were recently passed in Arizona and Massachusetts, but the laws are scheduled to go into effect for the 2002 elections.

In Massachusetts, to qualify for public funding under the new law candidates have to prove their viability by raising a minimum number of individual contributions of between $5 and $100 dollars. For example, gubernatorial candidates have to raise 6,000 such contributions while state representative candidates are required to obtain 200 contributions between $5 and $100, and state senate contenders need 400 qualifying contributions. The law sets a $100 contribution limit, bans unlimited transfers of soft money from national to state political parties, and requires timely Internet electronic disclosure of all contributions to candidates and political committees.

Like Minnesota, the law provides matching funds to participating candidates over and above the amount for which they are eligible if they face a nonparticipating opponent. Finally, unlike the Massachusetts Clean Money law, Maine adopted a law similar to Minnesota's to address independent expenditures. The First Circuit Federal Court of Appeals upheld the law, creating a split in the Circuit Courts over the constitutionality of laws regulating independent expenditures.

## Conclusion

States display many creative ways of addressing the growing impact of money on politics. The lesson from their experiences is that mere disclosure is not enough and that some form of public financing of campaigns and elections, coupled with regulation of soft money, independent expenditures, and lobbyist behavior is required if people are to take back their government.

*David Schultz is professor in the Graduate School of Public Administration and Management at Hamline University, St. Paul, Minnesota. He is author and editor of numerous articles and books on money and politics, including* Money, Politics, and Campaign Finance Reform Law in the States, *as well as past president and lobbyist for Common Cause Minnesota.*

# ORDERING INFORMATION

MAIL ORDERS TO:
Jossey-Bass
989 Market Street
San Francisco, CA 94103-1741

PHONE subscription or single-copy orders toll-free to (888) 378-2537 or to (415) 433-1767 (toll call).

FAX orders toll-free to (800) 481-2665.

SUBSCRIPTIONS cost $55.00 for individuals U.S./Canada/Mexico; $105.00 for U.S. institutions, agencies, and libraries; $145.00 for Canada institutions; $179.00 for international institutions. Standing orders are accepted. (For subscriptions outside the United States, orders must be prepaid in U.S. dollars by check drawn on a U.S. bank or charged to VISA, MasterCard, American Express, or Discover.)

SINGLE COPIES cost $25.00 plus shipping (see below) when payment accompanies order. Please include appropriate sales tax. Canadian residents, add GST and any local taxes. Billed orders will be charged shipping and handling. No billed shipments to Post Office boxes. (Orders from outside the United States must be prepaid in U.S. dollars drawn on a U.S. bank or charged to VISA, MasterCard, or American Express.)

Prices are subject to change without notice.

| SHIPPING (single copies only): | Surface | Domestic | Canadian |
|---|---|---|---|
| | First item | $5.00 | $6.00 |
| | Each add'l item | $3.00 | $1.50 |

For next-day, second-day, and international delivery rates, call the number provided above.

ALL ORDERS must include either the name of an individual or an official purchase order number. Please submit your orders as follows:
  *Subscriptions:* specify issue (for example, NCR 86:1) you would like subscription to begin with.
  *Single copies:* specify volume and issue number. Available from Volume 86 onward. For earlier issues, see below.

MICROFILM available from University Microfilms, 300 North Zeeb Road, Ann Arbor, MI 48106. Back issues through Volume 85 and bound volumes available from William S. Hein & Co., 1285 Main Street, Buffalo, NY 14209. Full text available in the electronic versions of the Social Sciences Index, H. W. Wilson Co., 950 University Avenue, Bronx, NY 10452, and in CD-ROM from EBSCO Publishing, 83 Pine Street, P.O. Box 2250, Peabody, MA 01960. The full text of individual articles is available via fax modem through Uncover Company, 3801 East Florida Avenue, Suite 200, Denver, CO 80210. For bulk reprints (50 or more), call David Famiano, Jossey-Bass, at (415) 433-1740.

DISCOUNTS FOR QUANTITY ORDERS are available. For information, please write to Jossey-Bass, 989 Market Street, San Francisco, CA 94103-1741.

LIBRARIANS are encouraged to write to Jossey-Bass for a free sample issue.

VISIT THE JOSSEY-BASS HOME PAGE on the World Wide Web at http://www.josseybass.com for an order form or information about other titles of interest.

ALL PRICES include shipping and handling (for orders outside the United States, please add $15 for shipping). National Civic League members receive a 10 percent discount. Bulk rates are available. See end of this list for ordering information.

## Most Frequently Requested Publications

*The Civic Index: A New Approach to Improving Community Life*
National Civic League staff, 1993
50 pp., 7 × 10 paper, $7.00

*The Community Visioning and Strategic Planning Handbook*
National Civic League staff, 1995
53 pp., $23.00

## Governance

*National Report on Local Campaign Finance Reform*
New Politics Program staff, 1998
96 pp., $15.00

*Communities and the Voting Rights Act*
National Civic League staff, 1996
118 pp., 8.5 × 11 paper, $12.00

*Forms of Local Government*
National Civic League staff, 1993
15 pp., 5.5 × 8.5 pamphlet, $3.00

*Guide for Charter Commissions (Fifth Edition)*
National Civic League staff, 1991
46 pp., 6 × 9 paper, $10.00

*Handbook for Council Members in Council-Manager Cities (Fifth Edition)*
National Civic League staff, 1992
38 pp., 6 × 9 paper, $12.00

*Measuring City Hall Performance: Finally, A How-To Guide*
Charles K. Bens, 1991
127 pp., 8.5 × 11 monograph, $15.00

*Model County Charter (Revised Edition)*
National Civic League staff, 1990
53 pp., 5.5 × 8.5 paper, $10.00

*Modern Counties: Professional Management—The Non-Charter Route*
National Civic League staff, 1993
54 pp., paper, $8.00

*Term Limitations for Local Officials: A Citizen's Guide to Constructive Dialogue*
Laurie Hirschfeld Zeller, 1992
24 pp., 5.5 × 8.5 pamphlet, $3.00

*Using Performance Measurement in Local Government: A Guide to Improving Decisions, Performance, and Accountability*
Paul D. Epstein, 1988
225 pp., 6 × 9 paper, $5.00

*Model City Charter (Seventh Edition)*
National Civic League staff, 1997
110 pp., 5.5 × 8.5 monograph, $14.00

## Alliance for National Renewal

*ANR Community Resource Manual*
National Civic League Staff, 1996
80 pp., 8.5 × 11, $6.00

*Taking Action: Building Communities That Strengthen Families*
Special section in *Governing Magazine,* 1998
8 pp., 8.5 × 11 (color), $3.00

*Communities That Strengthen Families*
Insert in *Governing Magazine,* 1997
8 pp., 8.5 × 11 reprint, $3.00

*Connecting Government and Neighborhoods*
Insert in *Governing Magazine,* 1996
8 pp., 8.5 × 11 reprint, $3.00

*The Culture of Renewal*
Richard Louv, 1996
45 pp., $8.00

*The Kitchen Table*
Quarterly newsletter of Alliance for National Renewal, 1999
8 pp., annual subscription (4 issues) $12.00, free to ANR Partners

*The Landscape of Civic Renewal*
Civic renewal projects and studies from around the country, 1999
185 pp., $12.00

*National Renewal*
John W. Gardner, 1995
27 pp., 7 × 10, $7.00

*San Francisco Civic Scan*
Richard Louv, 1996
100 pp., $6.00

*1998 Guide to the Alliance for National Renewal*
National Civic League staff, 1998
50 pp., 4 × 9, $5.00

*Springfield, Missouri: A Nice Community Wrestles with How to Become a Good Community*
Alliance for National Renewal staff, 1996
13 pp., $7.00

*Toward a Paradigm of Community-Making*
Allan Wallis, 1996
60 pp., $12.00

*The We Decade: Rebirth on Community*
*Dallas Morning News*, 1995
39 pp., 8.5 × 14 reprint, $3.00

*99 Things You Can Do for Your Community in 1999*
poster (folded), $6.00

## Healthy Communities

*Healthy Communities Handbook*
National Civic League staff, 1993
162 pp., 8.5 × 11 monograph, $22.00

## All-America City Awards

*All-America City Yearbook (1991, 1992, 1993, 1994, 1995, 1996, 1997)*
National Civic League staff
60 pp., 7 × 10 paper, $4.00 shipping and handling

*All-America City Awards Audio Tape Briefing*
Audiotape, $4.00 shipping and handling

## Diversity and Regionalism

*Governance and Diversity:*
*Findings from Oakland, 1995*
*Findings from Fresno, 1995*
*Findings from Los Angeles, 1994*
National Civic League staff
7 × 10 paper, $5.00 each

*Networks, Trust and Values*
Allan D. Wallis, 1994
51 pp., 7 × 10 paper, $7.00

*Inventing Regionalism*
Allan D. Wallis, 1995
75 pp., 8.5 × 11 monograph, $19.00

## Leadership, Collaboration, and Community Building

*Citistates: How Urban America Can Prosper in a Competitive World*
Neal Peirce, Curtis Johnson, and John Stuart Hall, 1993
359 pp., 6.5 × 9.5, $25.00

*Collaborative Leadership*
David D. Chrislip and Carl E. Larson, 1994
192 pp., 6 × 9.5, $20.00

*Good City and the Good Life*
Daniel Kemmis, 1995
226 pp., 6 × 8.5, $23.00

*On Leadership*
  John W. Gardner, 1990
  220 pp., 6 × 9.5, $28.00

*Politics for People: Finding a Responsible Public Voice*
  David Mathews, 1994
  229 pp., 6 × 9.5, $20.00

*Public Journalism and Public Life*
  David "Buzz" Merritt, 1994
  129 pp., 6 × 9, $30.00

*Resolving Municipal Disputes*
  David Stiebel, 1992
  2 audiotapes and book, $15.00

*Time Present, Time Past*
  Bill Bradley, former chairman of the National Civic League, 1996
  450 pp., paper, $13.00

*Transforming Politics*
  David D. Chrislip, 1995
  12 pp., 7 × 10, $3.00

*Revolution of the Heart*
  Bill Shore, 1996
  167 pp., 8.5 × 5.75, $8.00

*The Web of Life*
  Richard Louv, 1996
  258 pp., 7.5 × 5.5, $15.00

### Programs for Community Problem Solving

*Systems Reform and Local Government: Improving Outcomes for Children, Families, and Neighborhoods*
  1998, 47 pp., $12.00

*Building Community: Exploring the Role of Social Capital and Local Government*
  1998, 31 pp., $12.00

*The Transformative Power of Governance: Strengthening Community Capacity to Improve Outcomes for Children, Families, and Neighborhoods*
  1998, 33 pp., $12.00

*Building the Collaborative Community*
  Jointly published by the National Civic League and the National Institute for Dispute Resolution, 1994
  33 pp., $12.00

*Negotiated Approaches to Environmental Decision Making in Communities: An Exploration of Lessons Learned*
  Jointly published by the National Institute for Dispute Resolution and the Coalition to Improve Management in State and Local Government, 1996
  58 pp., $14.00

*Community Problem Solving Case Summaries, Volume III*
  1992, 52 pp., $19.00

*Facing Racial and Cultural Conflicts: Tools for Rebuilding Community (Second Edition)*
  1994, $24.00

*Collaborative Transportation Planning Guidelines for Implementing ISTEA and the CAAA*
  1993, 87 pp., $14.00

*Collaborative Planning Video*
  Produced by the American Planning Association, 1995
  6-hr. video and 46 pp. workshop materials, $103.00

*Pulling Together: A Land Use and Development Consensus Building Manual*
  A joint publication of PCPS and the Urban Land Institute, 1994
  145 pp., $34.00

*Solving Community Problems by Consensus*
  1990, 20 pp., $14.00

*Involving Citizens in Community Decision Making: A Guidebook*
  1992, 30 pp., $30.00

NATIONAL CIVIC LEAGUE sales policies: Orders must be paid in advance by check, VISA, or MasterCard. We are unable to process exchanges, returns, credits, or refunds. For orders outside the United States, add $15 for shipping.

TO PLACE AN ORDER:

CALL the National Civic League at (303) 571–4343 or (800) 223–6004, or

MAIL ORDERS TO:
  National Civic League
  1445 Market Street, Suite 300
  Denver, CO 80202–1717, or

E-MAIL the National Civic League at ncl@ncl.org